OPPOSING
VIEWPOINTS®
SERIES

Racial Profiling

Other Books of Related Interest:

Opposing Viewpoints Series
Human Rights

Terrorism

At Issue Series
National Security

Should Governments Negotiate with Terrorists?

Current Controversies Series
Homeland Security

Middle East

Introducing Issues with Opposing Viewpoints Series
Hate Crimes

Issues That Concern You Series
Discrimination

"Congress shall make no law. . .abridging the freedom of speech, or of the press."

First Amendment to the U.S. Constitution

The basic foundation of our democracy is the First Amendment guarantee of freedom of expression. The *Opposing Viewpoints* Series is dedicated to the concept of this basic freedom and the idea that it is more important to practice it than to enshrine it.

OPPOSING VIEWPOINTS® SERIES

Racial Profiling

David Erik Nelson, Book Editor

GREENHAVEN PRESS
A part of Gale, Cengage Learning

GALE
CENGAGE Learning·

Detroit • New York • San Francisco • New Haven, Conn • Waterville, Maine • London

Christine Nasso, *Publisher*
Elizabeth Des Chenes, *Managing Editor*

© 2009 Greenhaven Press, a part of Gale, Cengage Learning

Cover image © Dale Higgins / Workbook Stock / Jupiterimages.

LIBRARY OF CONGRESS CATALOGING-IN-PUBLICATION DATA

Racial profiling / David Erik Nelson, book editor.
    p. cm. -- (Opposing viewpoints)
Includes bibliographical references and index.
ISBN 978-0-7377-4222-0 (hardcover)
ISBN 978-0-7377-4223-7 (pbk.)
1. Racial profiling in law enforcement. 2. Discrimination in law enforcement. I.
Nelson, David Erik.
    HV7936.R3R323 2009
    363.2'3089--dc22
                                                                2008039335

Printed in the United States of America
 2 3 4 5 6   13 12 11 10 09

ED262

Contents

Chapter 4: What Are the Consequences of Racial Profiling?

Why Consider Opposing Viewpoints?

> "The only way in which a human being can make some approach to knowing the whole of a subject is by hearing what can be said about it by persons of every variety of opinion and studying all modes in which it can be looked at by every character of mind. No wise man ever acquired his wisdom in any mode but this."
>
> *John Stuart Mill*

In our media-intensive culture it is not difficult to find differing opinions. Thousands of newspapers and magazines and dozens of radio and television talk shows resound with differing points of view. The difficulty lies in deciding which opinion to agree with and which "experts" seem the most credible. The more inundated we become with differing opinions and claims, the more essential it is to hone critical reading and thinking skills to evaluate these ideas. *Opposing Viewpoints* books address this problem directly by presenting stimulating debates that can be used to enhance and teach these skills. The varied opinions contained in each book examine many different aspects of a single issue. While examining these conveniently edited opposing views, readers can develop critical thinking skills such as the ability to compare and contrast authors' credibility, facts, argumentation styles, use of persuasive techniques, and other stylistic tools. In short, the *Opposing Viewpoints* Series is an ideal way to attain the higher-level thinking and reading skills so essential in a culture of diverse and contradictory opinions.

In addition to providing a tool for critical thinking, *Opposing Viewpoints* books challenge readers to question their own strongly held opinions and assumptions. Most people form their opinions on the basis of upbringing, peer pressure, and personal, cultural, or professional bias. By reading carefully balanced opposing views, readers must directly confront new ideas as well as the opinions of those with whom they disagree. This is not to simplistically argue that everyone who reads opposing views will—or should—change his or her opinion. Instead, the series enhances readers' understanding of their own views by encouraging confrontation with opposing ideas. Careful examination of others' views can lead to the readers' understanding of the logical inconsistencies in their own opinions, perspective on why they hold an opinion, and the consideration of the possibility that their opinion requires further evaluation.

Evaluating Other Opinions

To ensure that this type of examination occurs, *Opposing Viewpoints* books present all types of opinions. Prominent spokespeople on different sides of each issue as well as well-known professionals from many disciplines challenge the reader. An additional goal of the series is to provide a forum for other, less known, or even unpopular viewpoints. The opinion of an ordinary person who has had to make the decision to cut off life support from a terminally ill relative, for example, may be just as valuable and provide just as much insight as a medical ethicist's professional opinion. The editors have two additional purposes in including these less known views. One, the editors encourage readers to respect others' opinions—even when not enhanced by professional credibility. It is only by reading or listening to and objectively evaluating others' ideas that one can determine whether they are worthy of consideration. Two, the inclusion of such viewpoints encourages the important critical thinking skill of objectively evaluating an author's credentials and bias. This evaluation will illuminate an author's reasons for taking a particular stance on an issue and will aid in readers' evaluation of the author's ideas.

It is our hope that these books will give readers a deeper understanding of the issues debated and an appreciation of the complexity of even seemingly simple issues when good and honest people disagree. This awareness is particularly important in a democratic society such as ours in which people enter into public debate to determine the common good. Those with whom one disagrees should not be regarded as enemies but rather as people whose views deserve careful examination and may shed light on one's own.

Thomas Jefferson once said that "difference of opinion leads to inquiry, and inquiry to truth." Jefferson, a broadly educated man, argued that "if a nation expects to be ignorant and free ... it expects what never was and never will be." As individuals and as a nation, it is imperative that we consider the opinions of others and examine them with skill and discernment. The *Opposing Viewpoints* Series is intended to help readers achieve this goal.

David L. Bender and Bruno Leone,
Founders

Introduction

"We were looking for a white van with white people, and we ended up with a blue car with black people."

—*Washington, DC,*
police chief Charles Ramsey, on how
the Beltway Snipers eluded arrest.

On September 6, 1901, Leon Czolgosz (pronounced "sholegosh"), an unemployed, Michigan-born anarchist and occasional factory worker, shot President William McKinley twice at point-blank range, causing injuries that resulted in the president's death eight days later.

It was a stifling early September afternoon and the president was greeting the public in the Temple of Music at the magnificent Pan-American Exposition in Buffalo, New York. Secret Service agent George Foster, stationed at the president's side, had noticed Czolgosz in the receiving line and found the nervous young man suspicious: his "pale complexion" was notable on a day when everyone else was sweating and flushed with the heat. Regrettably, the president's bodyguards quickly dismissed Czolgosz as nothing more than "a mechanic out for a day at the exposition." Like the other Secret Service agents, Foster was more concerned by the "big Negro" standing in line behind Czolgosz. Because the security detail was distracted by this hulking African American, Czolgosz was able to get to the head of the receiving line, a .32 revolver poorly concealed beneath a makeshift handkerchief bandage. When the president reached out to shake the anarchist's hand, Czolgosz pulled the trigger.

As it turns out, the very large African American man who had so distracted the Secret Service was James Parker, a former constable. When Czolgosz opened fire, Parker pounced on him, punching the assassin in the face and causing his second shot to miss its mark, grazing McKinley instead of piercing him. Parker then disarmed Czolgosz, who later confessed "I would have shot more but I was stunned by a blow in the face, a frightful blow that knocked me down and then everybody jumped on me!" Parker's quick action is credited with having extended the president's life by more than a week. Ironically, James Parker likely saved Czolgosz's life as well—for the moment, anyway. The enraged crowd immediately seized the anarchist and was set to lynch him on the spot; but McKinley, still alive because of Parker's quick action, commanded the crowd not to hurt the assassin. Czolgosz was taken into custody, found guilty at trial, and ultimately executed.

There's every indication that, had McKinley's guards not been distracted by their unwarranted suspicion of Parker, they would have apprehended Czolgosz before he fired: two days earlier, as McKinley arrived in Buffalo by train, Czolgosz had been in the crowd on the train station platform, waiting to greet him. As Czolgosz, already armed, pushed to the front of the crowd, an astute officer noticed the scuffle. The officer moved down the platform to investigate, spoiling Czolgosz's opportunity.

Unfortunately, it doesn't appear that Americans have learned anything from this historical footnote. Seventy-four years later, almost to the day, Lynette "Squeaky" Fromme came within a hair's breadth of assassinating President Gerald Ford. Three weeks later, Sara Jane Moore made her own attempt. At the time, women didn't fit the profile of potential presidential assassins, and thus neither woman was considered a threat until she pulled out a pistol. In the autumn of 2002, the "Beltway Sniper" killed nearly a dozen people in the Washington, D.C., area. Police were so obsessed with early, confused eyewitness reports that gave descriptions fitting the stereotypical profile of a serial killer (a lone, white male) that the actual attackers (two African American men, John Allen Muhammad and Lee Boyd Malvo) were able to leave the scenes of the murders, slipping through police roadblocks multiple times while still armed with the murder weapon.

History and popular culture are rife with anecdotes like these. But for every black serial killer who is brought in for questioning and then released because "all serial killers are lonely white men," and for every presidential assassin who is helped, rather than hindered, by the profile, there are thousands of African Americans who feel they've been pulled over and searched for no greater crime than "driving while black," and hundreds of Muslim Americans who learn that their houses of worship are under surveillance and their charities are being monitored. The contributors to *Opposing Viewpoints: Racial Profiling* examine the many strange facets of racial profiling. They explore these in four chapters: Does Racial Profiling Exist? Should Arab Muslims Be Profiled in the War on Terror? Is Racial Profiling Generally Justifiable? and What Are the Consequences of Racial Profiling? Despite the enormous number of personal stories and daily tragedies that hinge on racial profiling, there is surprisingly little consensus as to whether a racial profiling problem even exists, what the exact dimensions of that problem might be, and what its repercussions are.

OPPOSING
VIEWPOINTS®
SERIES

CHAPTER 1

Does Racial Profiling Exist?

Chapter Preface

A mericans take it as a given that racial profiling is pervasive in the United States, and is in fact so common that shorthand references to it are the basis of jokes, such as "driving while black" or "flying while Muslim." Racial profiling was perceived as such a major problem in the United States, and as such an embarrassing stain on the national character, that one of President George W. Bush's first initiatives upon taking office in 2001 was to address a joint session of Congress to make clear that his administration would put an end to racial profiling in America. This being the case, it may come as a surprise to learn that no large-scale empirical studies have been able to demonstrate widespread use of racial profiling by law enforcement. Some smaller studies, such as one examining drug enforcement by Maryland state troopers, actually found that those troopers were pulling over and searching *too few* minority members. This, of course, flies in the face of experience: almost every person of color in America can offer a personal story about his or her own experience of being singled out by a police officer, security guard, or business owner solely on the basis of race.

Nonetheless, even though the existence of racial profiling is hotly debated, no one questions the profound impact that the perception of racial profiling has on the lives of average Americans. The broad perception that law enforcement officers regularly decide to stop, search, and even arrest people based solely on their perceived race or nationality is a constant source of stress for African Americans, Asian Americans, Latinos, and people of Middle Eastern descent. This stress itself strains relationships between law enforcement and minority communities, making the job of law enforcement that much more difficult.

The authors of the following viewpoints explore the existence of racial profiling in the United States and beyond, and discuss the various forms it might take.

"*Many racial profiling victims walk away with traffic tickets, but too often for others the outcome of racial profiling is death.*"

Racial Profiling Exists

American Civil Liberties Union

In the following viewpoint, the American Civil Liberties Union (ACLU) argues that racial profiling is pervasive in the United States and offers anecdotes demonstrating inappropriate profiling practices used by both law enforcement and private businesses. The ACLU believes these practices affect a large spectrum of minority groups, including African Americans, Native Americans, Latinos, and persons of Asian descent. The ACLU is dedicated to protecting all civil liberties guaranteed by the Bill of Rights, with a special focus on protecting the rights of disempowered groups.

As you read, consider the following questions:

1. How many shots were fired at Amadou Diallo, an unarmed African immigrant, by New York City police officers on February 4, 1999?

American Civil Liberties Union, *Racial Profiling: Definition*, www.aclu.org, November 23, 2005. Reproduced by permission.

2. According to a 1999 report, although New York City's population was only 25.6 percent African American, what percentage of the people stopped by the New York Police Department's Street Crime Unit were black?

3. During the 2000 elections in Florida, how many times more likely was an African American's ballot to be rejected than a white voter's ballot?

"Racial Profiling" refers to the discriminatory practice by law enforcement officials of targeting individuals for suspicion of crime based on the individual's race, ethnicity, religion or national origin. Criminal profiling, generally, as practiced by police, is the reliance on a group of characteristics they believe to be associated with crime. Examples of racial profiling are the use of race to determine which drivers to stop for minor traffic violations (commonly referred to as "driving while black or brown"), or the use of race to determine which pedestrians to search for illegal contraband.

Another example of racial profiling is the targeting, ongoing since the [2001] September 11th attacks, of Arabs, Muslims and South Asians for detention on minor immigrant violations in the absence of any connection to the attacks on the World Trade Center or the Pentagon.

[A] law enforcement agent [is defined as] a person acting in a policing capacity for public or private purposes. This includes security guards at department stores, airport security agents, police officers, or, more recently, airline pilots who have ordered passengers to disembark from flights, because the passengers' ethnicity aroused the pilots' suspicions. Members of each of these occupations have been accused of racial profiling.

Defining Racial Profiling

Racial profiling does not refer to the act of a law enforcement agent pursuing a suspect in which the specific description of the suspect includes race or ethnicity in combination with other identifying factors.

Defining racial profiling as relying "solely" on the basis of race, ethnicity, national origin or religion can be problematic. This definition found in some state racial profiling laws is unacceptable, because it fails to include when police act on the basis of race, ethnicity, national origin or religion in combination with an alleged violation of [a] law. Under the "solely" definition, an officer who targeted Latino drivers who were speeding would not be racial profiling because the drivers were not stopped "solely" because of their race but also because they were speeding. This would eliminate the vast majority of racial profiling now occurring.

Any definition of racial profiling must include, in addition to racially or ethnically discriminatory acts, *discriminatory omissions* on the part of law enforcement as well. For example, during the eras of lynching in the [American] South in the 19th and early 20th centuries and the civil rights movement in the 1950's and 1960's, southern sheriffs sat idly by while racists like the Ku Klux Klan [a white supremicist organization most prominent in the American South] terrorized African Americans. At times, the sheriffs would even release black suspects to the lynch mobs. A recent example would be the complaint by an African-American man in Maryland, who after moving into a white community, was attacked and subjected to property damage. Local police failed to respond to his repeated complaints until they arrested him for shooting his gun into the air, trying to disperse a hostile mob outside his home.

Racial Profiling May Be Hazardous to Your Health

Many racial profiling victims walk away with traffic tickets, but too often for others the outcome of racial profiling is death.

Pennsylvania (Brentwood)—On October 12, 1995, Jonny Gammage, a 31-year-old African-American male, was killed after being pulled over while driving the Jaguar of his cousin, Pittsburgh Steelers football player Ray Seals, in a predominantly white community. Although police claimed that Gammage initiated the struggle, a tow truck driver said he saw one officer start the fight and the others join in kicking, hitting and clubbing Gammage while he lay on the pavement. Three officers were tried for involuntary manslaughter: John Vojtas was acquitted; Lt. Milton Mulholland and Michael Albert had their charges dismissed after two mistrials. Gammage's family settled a wrongful death civil rights lawsuit against the five officers involved and their police departments for $1.5 million.

New York (Bronx-New York City)—On February 4, 1999, Amadou Diallo, an unarmed 22-year-old immigrant from New Guinea, West Africa, was shot and killed in the narrow vestibule of the apartment building where he lived. Four white officers, Sean Carroll, Kenneth Boss, Edward McMellon, and Richard Murphy, fired 41 bullets, hitting Diallo 19 times. All four were members of the New York City Police Department's Street Crimes Unit, which, under the slogan, "We Own the Night," used aggressive "stop and frisk" tactics against African Americans at a rate double that group's population percentage. A report on the unit by the state attorney general found that blacks were stopped at a rate 10 times that of whites, and that 35 percent of those stops lacked reasonable suspicion to detain or had reports insufficiently filled out to make a determination. Thousands attended Diallo's funeral. Demonstrations were held almost daily, along with the arrests of over 1,200 people in planned civil disobedience. In a trial that was moved out of the community where Diallo lived and to Albany in upstate New York, the four officers who killed Diallo were acquitted of all charges.

Ohio (Cincinnati)—On April 7, 2001, in the early morning hours, Timothy Thomas, a 19-year-old African American, was shot to death by police officer John Roach. Thomas had 14 outstanding misdemeanor warrants, mostly traffic violations,

23

including failure to wear a seat belt. According to a city councilman, he was running away, holding up his baggy pants, and
scaled a fence, landing in a driveway where Roach was ap-
proaching and shot Thomas. He became the fifth black male
in the city to die at the hands of police in a five-month period
and the fifteenth since 1995. Two nights of protests left broken
windows at City Hall and fires around the city. Witnesses reported that following Thomas' funeral, six city SWAT [special
weapons and tactics] team officers shot pellet-filled bags into
a peaceful crowd. Two people hit by the pellets filed lawsuits.
Under community and city council pressure, both the public
safety director and city manager resigned. Officer Roach was
indicted on charges of negligent homicide, and obstructing
official business, resulting from differences in his version of
events.

Roach was acquitted in a bench [non-jury] trial characterized by the judge's (a former prosecutor) open admiration for
Roach, and blaming Timothy Thomas for "making" Roach kill
him.

A community coalition, the Cincinnati Black United Front
and the ACLU of Ohio, filed suit against the city and the Fra-
ternal Order of Police, citing a pattern and practice of discrimination by police, including issuing the type of traffic ci-
tations Thomas received to African Americans at twice their
population percentage. In April 2002 the case was settled, under terms including the establishment of a civilian complaint
review board and the activation of the reporting of collected
traffic stop data that had been enacted by city ordinance in
2001. The [U.S.] Department of Justice also intervened and
settled with the city, including revision and review of [the police department's] use of force policy.

Race Influences the Use of Deadly Force

It is significant to note that research confirms the existence of
bias in decisions to shoot. A series of University of California/

Minority Users, Majority Arrests

Drug Use v. Drug Arrests

| | Crack cocaine | | Powder cocaine | |
Race	Percent of users	Percent of arrests	Percent of users	Percent of arrests
Whites	71.30%	5.70%	81.00%	18.20%
Blacks	17.70%	84.20%	7.70%	30.30%
Hispanics	7.90%	9.00%	8.50%	50.50%

TAKEN FROM: Statistics on drug use are from the National Household Survey on Drug Abuse (Substance Abuse and Mental Health Services Administration, 2000). Statistics on arrests for drug possession are from the Sourcebook of Federal Sentencing Statistics (U.S. Sentencing Commission 2000).

University of Chicago studies recreated the experience of a police officer confronted with a potentially dangerous suspect, and found that:

- participants fired on an armed target more quickly when the target was African American than when white, and decided not to shoot an unarmed target more quickly when the target was white than when African American

- participants failed to shoot an armed target more often when that target was white than when the target was African American. If the target was unarmed, participants mistakenly shot the target more often when African American than when white

- shooting bias was greater among participants who held a strong cultural stereotype of African Americans as aggressive, violent and dangerous, and among participants who reported more contact with African Americans. . . .

The stories above, and hundreds of others, present a compelling argument that not only does racial profiling exist, but it is widespread, and has had a destructive effect on the lives of communities of color, and attitudes toward police.

Racial Profiling of Asians

Asians, who, according to the U.S. census [the survey taken every ten years by a federal bureau devoted to that purpose], number 10 million, or 4 percent of the population, have been victims of racial profiling as well. Wen Ho Lee, a Taiwanese American was targeted and suspected of espionage on the basis of his race. Memos by high-ranking FBI [Federal Bureau of Investigation] and [U.S.] Department of Energy officials acknowledged that Lee was singled out because he was Chinese, and eight similarly situated non-Chinese were not prosecuted.

In Seattle, Washington in July 2001 a group of 14 Asian American youth were stopped by police for jaywalking, claiming that they were kept against the wall for about an hour. The *Seattle Times* reported that one officer told them he had visited their country while in the army, and asked them repeatedly whether they spoke English. The paper also reported that U.S. Representative David Wu (D-Oregon) was detained entering the headquarters of the Department of Energy repeatedly.

In 2001, the Asian Freedom Project of Wisconsin issued a report that found the racial profiling of Hmong [an ethnic group from the mountains of Southeast Asia] communities there, and included the testimony of adults, as well as boys and girls.

The Garden Grove (CA) Police Department settled a "gang" database racial profiling lawsuit by a group of young Asian Americans who said their civil rights were violated when officers photographed them as suspected gang members based merely on their ethnicity and clothing.

Racial Profiling of Native Americans

Indigenous people (Native Americans) call it "DWI," with a new twist: "Driving While Indian." According to the National American Indian Housing Council, there are 2.4 million Indians (including Eskimos and Aleuts) in the United States. Indians complain about stops and searches by local police and sheriffs on roads leading to and from reservations.

In South Dakota, widespread reports of racial profiling led to hearings before the state legislature, where Indians testified about their being stopped and searched not only based on race but also on religious articles hanging from rearview mirrors, and regional license plates that identified them as living on reservations.

In June 2002 scores of Indians in the state's Bennett County complained to [U.S.] Department of Justice attorneys, alleging racial profiling at the hands of sheriffs there, including vehicular stops in the absence of reasonable suspicion, the administration of breathalyzer tests without reasonable suspicion, warrantless searches of homes and vehicles, and demanding to see drivers licenses and vehicle registrations while inside bars.

Walking and Bicycling While Black and Brown

Although "Driving While Black/Brown" traffic stops and searches are the form of racial profiling that has received the most media attention, profiling takes place off the roadways as well. Black and Latino pedestrians are regularly stopped and frisked without reasonable cause.

In New York City, the December 1999 report of the New York City Police Department's pedestrian "stop and frisk" practices by the state attorney general provided glaring evidence of racial profiling in the nation's largest city. Blacks comprise 25.6 percent of the City's population, yet 50.6 percent of all persons "stopped" during the period were black.

Hispanics comprise 23.7 percent of the City's population yet, 33.0 percent of all "stops" were of Hispanics. By contrast, whites are 43.4 percent of the City's population, but accounted for only 12.9 percent of all stops. Blacks comprise 62.7 percent of all persons "stopped" by the NYPD's Street Crime Unit ("SCU").

In precincts in which blacks and Hispanics each represented less than 10 percent of the total population, individuals identified as belonging to these racial groups nevertheless accounted for more than half of the total "stops" during the covered period. Blacks accounted for 30 percent of all persons "stopped" in these precincts. Hispanics accounted for 23.4 percent of all persons "stopped."

Finally, precincts where minorities constitute the majority of the overall population tended to see more "stop and frisk" activity than precincts where whites constitute a majority of the population: Of the ten precincts showing the highest rate of "stop and frisk" activity (measured by "stops" per 1,000 residents), in only one (the 10th Precinct) was the majority of the population white. In seven other precincts, blacks and Hispanics constituted the majority of the population. The remaining two precincts were business districts in Manhattan and Brooklyn in which the daytime racial breakdown of persons within the precinct is unknown.

In roughly half of the police precincts in New York City, the majority of the population living in the precinct is white. However, of these 36 majority-white precincts, only 13 were in the top half of precincts showing most "stops" during the period. . . .

Youth of color have been victims of racially-motivated bicycling stops. In April 2001 the ACLU joined a suit against Eastpointe, Michigan, representing 21 young African-American men who were stopped by the police while riding their bikes there. The ACLU argued that the bicyclists were stopped in this predominantly white suburb of Detroit because of their race and not because they were doing anything wrong. In a 1996 memorandum to the Eastpointe City Manager, the former police chief stated that he instructed his officers to investigate any black youths riding through Eastpointe subdivisions. Police searched many of [the] young men and, in some cases, seized and later sold their bicycles. Police logs and reports in Eastpointe have identified over 100 incidents between 1995 and 1998 in which African-American youth were detained.

Discriminatory Use of Canine Units

A throwback to the grainy '60's black and white television news footage of vicious police dogs attacking peaceful black civil rights protesters is the continued discriminatory use of canine units by police. These dogs, lethal weapons capable of biting at 2,000 pounds pressure per square inch, and their handlers have been implicated in a vicious form of racial profiling that has led to legal action:

California (Los Angeles)—The ACLU of Southern California compiled reports on the hundreds of mostly blacks and Latinos who were bitten by Los Angeles Police Department dogs from 1990 to 1992, charging that the dogs trained to "attack and maul," were routinely sent out in non-violent situations. In 1997, California state highway patrol canine units stopped almost 34,000 vehicles. Only 2 percent were carrying drugs.

Maryland (Prince George's County)—The *Washington Post* reported that in May 2001 federal prosecutors charged a county police officer with releasing her police dog on an unarmed Mexican immigrant as part of a pattern of using and threatening the use of the dog on people of color. Despite being the subject of four lawsuits, twice being guilty of making false statements to a supervisor, and five prior instances of releasing the dog on suspects who weren't resisting, and being flagged by a departmental "early warning" system, the officer remained undisciplined in any substantive way. In 1999 the *Post* reported that thirteen police dog excessive force suits had been filed in Prince George's circuit and federal courts, in addition to five others that ended in judgment for plaintiffs or settlement. Of the total, ten alleged repeated bites of suspects once under police control, or while cuffed or on the ground.

South Dakota (Wagner)—While not involving the use of physical canine force, the issue reached a new low when school officials and police led a large German shepherd drug dog through classrooms in suspicionless drug searches of Yankton Sioux K-12 students, some as young as six years old. In July 2002, the ACLU filed suit in federal court.

Washington (Seattle)—In 1992 the ACLU alleged that police dog handlers used excessive force on suspects. Dogs were trained to attack and bite suspects regardless of their actions, even against alleged shoplifters, gasoline siphoners and jaywalkers. They also reported that in that year, 40 percent of police dog attacks were against African Americans, and that 91 people had received police dog bite injuries requiring hospitalization. . . .

Racial Profiling by Businesses

The targeting of shoppers/business patrons of color for suspicion of shoplifting by private security and other employees has disproportionately affected both working and prominent African-American women. TV talk show host Oprah Winfrey said she was refused buzz-in entry to a store even after seeing white women admitted and making a second attempt. After calling from a pay phone and being assured the store was in fact open, a third try failed as well. U.S. Congresswoman Maxine Waters said she was followed around a store and required to show her key at a hotel, unlike whites who entered before her. Professional basketball player and Olympic medalist Sheryl

Swoopes was kept waiting to be seated for almost an hour at a restaurant, while whites who arrived after her were seated before her.

Pauline Hampton and her niece, both African Americans, were shopping at the Dillard department store in Overland Park, Kansas, a suburb of Kansas City, with their children. After making several purchases, they went to the cosmetics counter to redeem a coupon. A white security guard accused Hampton of shoplifting, took her shopping bag, and, without consent, searched it, emptying the bag onto the counter. After finding the receipt for the items, he shoved the goods and the empty bag back to her. When she complained about his actions, the guard ordered them to leave, and threatened to call the police and have them forcibly removed. Hampton eventually called her husband to the scene and the situation escalated. They sued, and were awarded a $1.2 million judgment; the U.S. Supreme Court declined to hear Dillard's appeal.

The store chain, based in Arkansas, has also faced dozens of racial profiling lawsuits, claiming harassment and false arrest, in other states including Arkansas, Iowa, and Texas. Evidence produced in one case showed that although 16 percent of its shoppers were African American, 87 percent of the false arrest claims were made by them. In Texas, Dillard settled and paid money to the family of an African American customer who died at a store after being beaten and hog-tied while being detained, and has also settled discrimination suits by employees in Kansas and Missouri.

Other companies sued for racial profiling include Eddie Bauer, Avis Rent A Car, Denny's Restaurant, The Children's Place, and Holiday Spa.

Racial Profiling by the INS

The Immigration and Naturalization Service (INS) has had a history of disproportionately targeting ethnic groups of color for undocumented labor violations. Like all law enforcement,

INS agents must have sufficient evidence of wrongdoing to establish probable cause or reasonable suspicion to arrest or detain. They may not carry out their duties in a racially or ethnically discriminatory manner. While ethnicity or nationality are obviously critical elements in immigration violations by themselves, without additional facts there is insufficient basis for law enforcement action.

The New York Times reviewed files of INS raids released as part of the settlement of a garment workers union selective enforcement suit against the agency in New York City. The settlement included a summary that Latinos were 96 percent of the 2,907 people arrested in the 187 worksite raids carried out by the INS in the district, far greater than their representation in the city's legal or illegal population. This occurred even where the INS acknowledged that half the workers were not Latino but Asian, including undocumented immigrants.

And while some raids were based on informant information, 80 percent were initiated by agents who cited as primary evidence subjects' appearance or language without evidence of wrongdoing. Included were skin color, speaking Spanish or English with a Spanish accent, appearing to be of South or Central American descent and wearing clothing "not typical of North Americans." Such characterizations in major American cities are common to born and naturalized citizens alike.

Undocumented workers were discovered and arrested in all but a few of the reviewed raids, but nearly everyone arrested was Latino.

Racial Profiling by the INS Is Nationwide

Suits have also been filed in Arkansas, California, Louisiana, and Ohio claiming racial profiling by the INS. A federal court in Ohio found violations of the rights of Latinos by that state's highway patrol's practice of stopping Latino drivers to question them about their immigration status, including officers even confiscating the green cards of legal migrant workers claiming they were counterfeit. In California, federal courts have found Fourth Amendment [the U.S. Constitutional protection against unreasonable search and seizure] violations of Latinos in the stopping of Latinos on the basis of appearance and foreign sounding names.

The Supreme Court has held that INS agents working near the Mexican border may use Spanish ethnicity as a basis for detaining a person, but that it may not be the only basis.

A related issue is the targeting by police, first reported by the ACLU in Florida, of Latinos waiting on public sidewalks for labor employers to appear and select them for work, under the offense of being "visual clutter."

Racial Profiling at the Voting Booth

In Florida, the 2000 presidential election was rampant with claims of racial profiling. The presumption that African Americans tended to vote Democratic provided the Republican-controlled election apparatus with an easily identified target. The state changed the election's outcome by targeting people of color in a manner reminiscent of the racist poll taxes and literacy requirements of earlier Southern history. . . .

In the months before the election, Florida's secretary of state compiled an "ex-felon scrub list" of names for removal from the voter rolls [though it varies by state, convicted felons often do not have the right to vote]. It contained thousands of inexact matches as well as names of state residents with convictions in other states that turned out not to be felonies. These actions were destined to have a disparate impact on people of color because of their higher rate of incarceration. And, in an action with similar impact, Florida residents with felony convictions in other states were removed from the rolls, even though courts had previously ordered the reinstating of voting rights to all who would have been eligible to vote in the state of their conviction.

On election day, poll workers in communities of color, following elected officials' instructions to strictly challenge voter eligibility, required photo identification of African Americans while asking for none of whites, and required two forms of identification from Latinos where the law called for only one. Untold numbers, estimated to be in the thousands, were not given affidavit ballots that would preserve their votes pending resolution of any qualification issues. Even the state NAACP [National Association for the Advancement of Colored People] president was denied one until she stated her willingness to be jailed over the issue.

Most serious were the hundreds of reports, in African-American communities, of state police harassment of voters at polling places and traffic checkpoints, where they lined up cars, checking driving papers and inspecting vehicles. Racial profiling at its worst, this tactic appeared to be designed to delay and intimidate voters of color.

As to the ballot controversy, African Americans were 11 percent of the eligible voters, but 54 percent of the rejected ballots; four times more likely to have ballots rejected as white voters; more likely to be voting by punch card, which had three times higher error rates than optical-scan systems; and received almost none of the laptop computers sent to precincts for county voter registration record access.

Racial Profiling at the Airport

Airline passengers of color have long complained of racial profiling. [U.S.] Customs officials at international airports [who are responsible, among other things, for preventing the import of illegal substances] were found to have systematically targeted members of certain racial and ethnic groups, particularly black women, for intrusive and degrading personal searches, based on the false assumption that they were more likely to be transporting drugs.

In March 2000 the [U.S. government's] General Accounting Office issued a report of Customs searches of 102,000 airline passengers in [the] years 1997 and 1998. It found that black women were 9 times more likely than white women to be x-rayed after a frisk or pat-down search, but less than half as likely to be found carrying contraband. During those years, the *Washington Post* reported, 90 black women sued Customs after being searched at O'Hare Airport in Chicago, and one Hispanic woman, Amanda Buritica, sued after being stopped, handcuffed, placed in a hospital and forced to ingest powerful laxatives. When she was released 25 hours later, no drugs had been found.

A new commissioner, Ray Kelly, was brought in and pledged to end the practice. Although he eliminated the vague and often contradictory criteria that the agency used to decide who to stop, and although he reduced the total searches from 44,000 ('98) to 23,000 ('99) to 9,000 ('00), data from his own agency indicated that, despite his claims to the contrary, the search rate for African Americans increased dramatically, from 14 percent ('98) to 19 percent ('99) to 27 percent ('00).

> *"According to a survey of 80,000 civilians . . . in 2002, an identical proportion of white, black, and Hispanic drivers—9 percent—were stopped by the police in the previous year."*

Racial Profiling Does Not Exist

Heather Mac Donald

In the following viewpoint, Heather Mac Donald argues that reporting of widespread racial profiling is often inflated and misleading, which, she believes, contributes to an erroneous belief that profiling is pervasive, with negative repercussions throughout society. Heather Mac Donald is a fellow at the Manhattan Institute for Policy Research, a conservative think tank that supports economic choice and individual responsibility, and the author of Are Cops Racist? How the War Against the Police Harms Black Americans.

As you read, consider the following questions:

1. How does University of Toledo law professor David Harris define "driving while black"?

Heather Mac Donald, "Reporting While Wrong: *The New York Times* Peddles More 'Driving While Black' Malarkey," *National Review*, vol. 57, no. 17, September 26, 2005. Copyright © 2005 by National Review, Inc., 215 Lexington Avenue, New York, NY 10016. Reproduced by permission.

2. According to Mac Donald, what percentage of persons involved in a "force incident" admitted to verbally abusing or threatening the officer?

3. How does Mac Donald think exaggerated reporting of racial profiling hurts inner-city residents, regardless of their race?

The *New York Times*'s bad faith regarding the police has reached a new low. On August 24 [2005], a front-page article claimed that the [U.S.] Justice Department had tried to suppress damning evidence of racial profiling by the nation's police forces. In fact, it is the *Times* that is suppressing evidence.

The "Driving While Black" Myth

For years, activists have argued that some drivers face a heightened risk of being stopped by bigoted cops. David Harris, a University of Toledo law professor and ubiquitous police critic, provided a classic statement of the "Driving While Black" conceit in 1999: "Anyone who is African-American is automatically suspect during every drive to work, the store, or a friend's house." Owing to this "automatic suspicion," Harris posited in his 2002 book, *Profiles in Injustice*, "pretextual stops will be used against African-Americans and Hispanics . . . out of proportion to their numbers in the driving population."

The "Driving While Black" belief is pervasive, powerful, and false. According to a survey of 80,000 civilians conducted by the Bureau of Justice Statistics (BJS, an arm of the Justice Department) in 2002, an identical proportion of white, black, and Hispanic drivers—9 percent—were stopped by the police in the previous year. And the stop rate for blacks was lower during the day, when officers can more readily determine a driver's race, than at night. These results demolish the claim that minorities are disproportionately subject to "pretextual stops."

Clearly, these findings should be news of a high order—so that must be why the *Times* buried them in paragraph 11 of its front-page story (and omitted the day-night disparity entirely). But not only did the *Times* conceal the study's import, it also had the temerity to spin the survey as confirming the racial-profiling myth. Indeed, the BJS study will "add grist to the debate over using racial and ethnic data in law enforcement," the newspaper asserted, because it provided evidence of "the aggressive police treatment of black and Hispanic drivers."

What is this evidence for racist policing, in the paper's view? The *Times* bases its charge on two findings from the survey: According to driver self-reports, black and Hispanics were more likely to have their persons or cars searched than white drivers, and were more likely to be subjected to the threat or use of force by the officer who stopped them. The survey defines force as pushing, grabbing, or hitting; a typical force incident, characterized by the survey respondent as "excessive," consisted of an officer grabbing the respondent by the arm as he was fleeing the scene and pushing him against his car. Specifically, black drivers said that they or their cars were searched 10.2 percent of the time following a stop, Hispanic drivers 11.4 percent of the time, and white drivers 3.5 percent of the time. As for police threats or use of force, 2.4 percent of Hispanic drivers, 2.7 percent of black drivers, and 0.8 percent of white drivers claimed that force had been threatened or used against them.

Minority Drivers More Likely to Be Arrested

None of these findings establishes prejudicial treatment of minorities. The *Times*, for instance, does not reveal that blacks and Hispanics were far more likely to be arrested following a stop: Blacks were 11 percent of all stopped drivers, but 24 percent of all arrested drivers; Hispanics, 9.5 percent of all stopped drivers, but 18.4 percent of all arrested drivers; and whites, 76.5 percent of all stopped drivers, but 58 percent of arrested drivers. The higher black and Hispanic arrest rates undoubtedly result from their higher crime rates. The national black murder rate, for example, is seven times higher than that of all other races combined, and the black robbery rate eight times higher. Though the FBI [Federal Bureau of Investigation] does not keep national crime data on Hispanics, local police statistics usually put the Hispanic crime rate between the black and white crime rates. These differential crime rates mean that when the police run a computer search on black and Hispanic drivers following a stop, they are far more likely to turn up outstanding arrest warrants than for white drivers.

These higher arrest rates in turn naturally result in higher search rates: Officers routinely search civilians incident to an arrest. Moreover, the higher crime rates among blacks and Hispanics mean a greater likelihood that evidence of a crime, such as weapons or drugs, may be in plain view, thereby triggering an arrest and a search.

The higher incidence of police threats or use of force against blacks and Hispanics—assuming the self-reports are accurate—is also more likely to result from driver conduct than from police bias. Criminology studies have long found that the greatest predictor of police behavior is civilian behavior. Threaten or challenge an officer and you are likely to be challenged back. The 2002 BJS survey concluded that persons who provoked the police were significantly more likely to experience the threat or use of force by the officer than persons who did not. Thus, 24 percent of persons involved in a police force incident admitted to cursing at, insulting, or threatening the officer. The number of people who actually engaged in such behavior is probably higher still.

Driving While Speeding

The [New Jersey Turnpike] study used specially designed radar gun cameras, which are used to photograph the license plates of speeders and whose photos are accepted as evidence in many courts around the country, to capture images of drivers in a variety of locations on the turnpike. The study defined speeding as exceeding the speed limit by 15 miles per hour, and officers are instructed to focus on the most egregious speeders.

Researchers then showed the photos of 38,747 drivers to teams of three evaluators who tried to determine each driver's race, without knowing whether the driver had sped or not. At least two evaluators were able to agree on the race of 26,334 of the drivers photographed, and an analysis of those motorists found that the disparity [in speeding rates] between white and black drivers widened at higher speeds. . . .

Those results startled officials in the state attorney general's office, who had assumed that the radar study would bolster their case that profiling was widespread. Instead, the study concluded that blacks make up 16 percent of the drivers on the turnpike and 25 percent of the speeders in the 65 m.p.h. zones, where complaints of profiling have been most common.

David Kocieniewski,
New York Times, *March 21, 2002.*

More Likely to Resist Arrest?

Speculatively speaking, it is likely that a greater percentage of blacks and Hispanics challenged or threatened a police officer than did whites. Why? Because for the last decade and a half, blacks and Hispanics have been fed a steady diet of police-racism stories. They have been told again and again that if an officer stops them, it is because of their race, not their conduct. Police officers have come to expect that the first words out of a black driver's mouth following a traffic stop will be, "You only stopped me because I'm black." The chance that such an attitude will escalate into more hostile behavior is much greater than zero. In addition, the differential crime rates mean that a higher proportion of black and Hispanic drivers will have a crime in their past that could lead them to resist the officer making the stop.

The BJS authors explicitly disavowed the possibility of using the survey data to conclude that driver race, rather than conduct, resulted in different search or force rates. The *Times*, however, shows no such reluctance. After belatedly acknowledging the identical stop rates among different racial and ethnic groups, the paper hastens to add that "what happened once the police made a stop differed markedly depending on race and ethnicity." The *Times* then goes on to posit a Bush administration cover-up of these allegedly compromising findings. According to the *Times*'s narrative, political appointees in the Justice Department demoted the Bureau of Justice Statistics director, Lawrence Greenfeld, after he refused to delete references to the differential search . . . rates from a press release announcing the 2002 survey. And in a further manifestation of political meddling, per the paper, the Justice Department opted not to issue the contested press release at all, but simply posted the report online—as it has done for nearly 70 percent of the reports released in 2004 and 2005. That was another detail not disclosed in the *Times*'s story.

The "Racial Profiling" Myth Damages Urban Life

So what? A press release that focused on the search and arrest rates would be seriously misleading. Yet the *Times*'s fake scoop produced the usual reaction: eager mimicry. Within 24 hours, news outlets ranging from National Public Radio to the *St. Petersburg* [Florida] *Times* had reproduced the story. One career cop-basher, Rep. John Conyers of Michigan, called for a congressional investigation into the alleged "cover-up." And the NAACP [National Association for the Advancement of Colored People] claimed that the study confirmed the "truth about racial profiling."

The notion that the police target blacks and Hispanics because of their skin color has damaged urban life. Thanks to racial-data-collection mandates, every officer knows that if he has "too many" interactions with minority citizens—including responding to crime calls or preventing a mugging—he could face a bias charge. Some officers will decide that it's wiser for their careers not to fight crime aggressively, leaving law-abiding inner-city residents at the mercy of thugs. The drumbeat against the cops increases the hostility against them, poisoning the trust needed for the most effective police work. The *New York Times*'s endless crusade against phantom police racism ensures that the poorest neighborhoods will continue to be held back by fear and violence.

> *"The fact remains that data collection in its present form is largely unreliable as a means to identify racial profiling."*

It Is Difficult to Establish Whether Racial Profiling Is Occurring

Steve Holbert and Lisa Rose

In the following viewpoint, Steve Holbert and Lisa Rose examine the complexity of the data collection and analysis necessary to determine whether officers are practicing racial profiling. The authors ultimately question whether it is possible to detect racial profiling solely by analyzing data on local demographics and traffic stops. Law enforcement veteran Steve Holbert and attorney Lisa Rose have written extensively on racial profiling among law enforcement officers and are coauthors of The Color of Guilt and Innocence: Racial Profiling and Police Practices in America.

As you read, consider the following questions:

　1. According to Holbert and Rose, what two factors must be proven to establish that racial profiling is occurring?

Steve Holbert and Lisa Rose, "Making Sense of the Data: The Shortcomings of Racial Profiling Data Collection and Analysis," *Law Enforcement Technology*, vol. 33, no. 7, July 2006. Copyright © 2006 Cygnus Business Media. All rights reserved. Reproduced by permission.

2. Why do the authors compare the different rate of seat-belt use among white and African-American drivers?

3. Why are census data a poor benchmark for establishing the appropriate number of traffic stops for various minority groups?

Imagine the reaction if a "mind reading machine" were invented and used as a means to weed out officers engaging in racial profiling on the street. What if this system could "detect" racism? The fact is, such technology does exist, and it's used regularly in law enforcement to screen potential candidates for employment. Though the polygraph examination has some valuable uses in law enforcement, any implication for use as a discrimination-detecting device would undoubtedly be highly controversial. Absent such a device, however, any attempt to second guess an officer's true motives in his or her contacts with the public will remain elusive, even in the face of the most stringent and sophisticated data collection system.

The Dangers of Sloppy Studies

Collecting data to determine whether an organization is engaging in racial profiling is daunting. Racial profiling continues to challenge law enforcement across the country, particularly in light of the expansion of officers' roles as immigration enforcers. As such, data collection efforts by law enforcement have become one of the most controversial issues surrounding racial profiling. To collect or not to collect? What will it prove? Is it accurate? Is it a deterrent, a burden or neither? Despite these often unanswered questions, collection efforts have skyrocketed in the past few years. The response by law enforcement has been mixed, as these studies are often designed to place blame at the back end of the system once the alleged discrimination has occurred, rather than operating at the front of the system to prevent the problem altogether. Though these studies may be considered definitive by some, those in law enforcement know that data can't tell us anything we don't already know. Most law enforcement leaders will agree that the most accurate assessment of police contacts with the public comes from looking at the values within the organization, those of its individual officers, and reaching out to establish dialogue with members of the community.

Though not wholly opposed to data collection, such efforts can be damaging to an organization if not done correctly. As it stands presently, very few, if any, of these efforts are scientifically based, nor designed to conclusively determine whether racial profiling is occurring. All too often, however, these studies are confused with a scientific analysis. Unlike a bona fide study with checks and balances, data collection has, in many cases, emerged as a "wolf in sheep's clothing," often haphazardly implemented with limited resources in an effort to appease the public and special interest groups. Though disparities in traffic stops do not in themselves prove racial profiling is occurring, organizations are forced to defend its officers when the public and media erroneously equate any variation in the data with racial profiling among the ranks.

Data Collection and Interpretation

In order to establish racial profiling, two factors must be proven, assuming all other things are equal. First, it must be demonstrated that blacks or Hispanics (or some other racial group) are no more likely than whites to violate traffic laws and, second, that police routinely pull over one of these minority groups at a higher rate than whites.

Though this approach may seem quite straightforward, no study has ever been conducted that objectively measures whether certain minority groups commit traffic and mechanical violations at a rate that is equal to whites.

It should be noted here that merely focusing on the "catch" rate will never truly tell us at what rate these violations occur among each racial group, as many of the violators may continue unchallenged. Absent the ability to definitively establish both of these factors, any data collection results are tainted even before the data is collected.

Data collection and data analysis are the two key components of any data collection system. Each of these components poses its own set of challenges for law enforcement administrators. Though no system has been deemed perfect, there are many pitfalls that can be avoided by taking a closer look at the fundamentals of these two areas.

Data Collection Is Tricky

When breaking down the collection process itself, two themes are paramount: First, the anonymity granted to the officers on the collection forms (in most jurisdictions); and secondly, the lack of independent checks and balances in many models. Even the most respected and sophisticated data collection studies reveal that the percentage of auto stops for which officers did not accurately fill out a data form is unknown. Some departments nationwide report that up to 50 percent of their traffic stops were not captured by a data collection system. Despite these shortcomings, these studies go forward and are reported to the public as "proof" that racial profiling is or is not occurring.

Largely contributing to flaws in the collection system is a factor difficult to predict or measure: the human factor. For example, in addition to officers failing to fill out collection forms or neglecting to fill them out accurately, they may also make a conscious decision to "regulate" the process in an effort to turn in favorable statistics, a phenomenon acknowledged in many traffic stop studies. It is difficult, if not impossible, to factor in these discretionary encounters, for example, those violators that could have been stopped, but weren't.

Another critical factor to consider is whether certain minority groups have a greater likelihood of being stopped for reasons other than race, with just one of these reasons being their own safety habits. For example, federal studies have shown that only 51 percent of blacks wear seatbelts versus 62 percent of whites. Assuming these statistics are consistent in states that have enacted mandatory seatbelt laws, blacks would be 11 percent more likely than whites to be stopped by police for this reason alone. Likewise, certain ethnic groups tend to equip and alter their vehicles so that they are distinguishable from non-altered vehicles. These vehicle alterations may also attract greater attention from law enforcement, resulting in a greater number of stops per capita.

The Challenges of Gathering Accurate Data

Undoubtedly the most controversial issue in terms of collecting data involves whether officers should be granted anonymity when filling out data collection cards. Though this issue is ripe for heated debate among administrators and police unions, the fact remains that absent effective checks and balances, the integrity of the numbers remains unreliable.

Though these variables pose some of the most daunting challenges to the data collection process, experts are exploring new ways to ensure that the data collected is as accurate as possible. Some of these efforts include substantial oversight and auditing by the organization or by an academic partner. These efforts also may be overseen by study facilitators, community leaders, and/or special interest groups. For example, data collection logs may be compared with in-car police video camera recordings or to police dispatch records in order to compare the details of each stop to what was recorded by the officer.

Others have developed internal supervisor audits of activity logs to identify areas of discrepancy. Though many of these oversight measures have improved the integrity of the data, law enforcement must continue to explore new and innovative approaches that will yield a level of accuracy and completeness such an important endeavor demands.

How Police Departments Try to Examine Profiling

[A 2000] study [by the St. Paul (Minnesota) Police Department] collected data from 41,249 traffic stops by asking questions in addition to the information routinely collected on the stops. The questions and possible answers were:

(1) Perceived race of individual stopped?: (W)hite, (B)lack, (H)ispanic, (A)sian or (N)ative American.

(2) Sex?: (F)emale or (M)ale.

(3) Was the driver frisked?: (Y)es or (N)o.

(4) Was the car searched?: (Y)es or (N)o.

The answers to the four questions were combined with general traffic stop source data used by the police department and generated a Summary Report for Traffic Stop Data. . . .

The department hired the Institute on Race and Poverty to analyze the data to determine whether the department engaged in racial profiling and if so, to suggest improvement that would allow for more comprehensive analysis of future data. . . .

The city argued that the driver's race and other information are incidental and the intended thrust of the study is the officer's perception of the race and color of the driver he was stopping, and what investigative tactics he or she employed based on that perception.

Barbara LeJones, Minnesota Lawyer, *May 19, 2003.*

Accurate data collection and stringent check-and-balance systems are crucial to the success of any data collection endeavor. It is important to remember that even the most rigid scientific data analysis will be inaccurate if the data it is based upon is flawed at the outset.

Data Interpretation Is Tricky

Once the data is collected, it must be analyzed to form sound conclusions. While some organizations choose to analyze data internally, others have turned to academic partners, statisticians, police research organizations, or private experts to assist in this complex process. Perhaps one of the most underutilized resources in this endeavor is the input of the line officer. Often, the line officer can educate command staff and academic partners about practical considerations that would not otherwise be apparent to those with limited or no street experience. It is often these considerations, however, that are overlooked and greatly compromise the integrity of the data analysis.

In many instances, for example, the race of the driver is impossible for the officer to discern prior to the stop. This may occur if the violation is observed at nighttime or at times of poor visibility, or when the officer is making the stop based solely on the reading from a radar detector. Likewise, many stops made by the officer may be initiated by the citizen, for example, roadway assistance, requests for directions or [for] officers to sign off on mechanical violations. Though the data from these stops may be accurate as a factual matter, they become critical components when trying to use the data to analyze whether the officer is engaging in racial profiling. It is important that organizations require officers to identify whether the race of the driver is discernible prior to the stop, and who initiated the stop, so that data from these contacts can be factored differently at the time of analysis.

Problems Establishing Benchmarks

Another key component is the establishment of a benchmark by which to gain meaning from these raw numbers. Many organizations currently use census data for comparing the racial demographics in the community to traffic stop data. When challenged statistically, however, census data cannot be considered an accurate benchmark against which to compare roadway demographics. This is because in most cases, population demographics vary substantially from roadway demographics. This logic suggests, for example, that if census figures report 5 percent of the population is African American, stops of African Americans in this jurisdiction should not exceed 5 percent. This logic if flawed for many reasons. First, the driving population may vary substantially from the residential population. Variables such as age are usually not factored in to the equation to determine the percentage of those of a particular ethnicity who are of driving age or who are licensed to drive. Census data also don't account for variables in census reporting such as margins of error, nor do they capture the number of people who may be commuting through the community who do not reside in the area.

Some experts have combined census data, DMV [department of motor vehicle] records of the driving public (where available and where race is included in these records), and roadway observations to determine the percentage of those people traveling in and out of the region. Though more accurate than census data alone, much more work needs to be done to develop a formula for establishing an accurate benchmark.

Even Perfect Data Collection and Analysis May Not Be Enough

The fact remains that data collection in its present form is largely unreliable as a means to identify racial profiling. This is simply because data will never reveal why an officer made one decision over another. For example, two officers in City X make a traffic stop. Everything about the stop is identical: the time of day, the vehicle, the gender, race and age of the driver.

In each instance, the driver is issued a citation for a broken taillight. The data recorded from these stops would be identical in every way.

Let's assume Officer A stopped the vehicle after noticing the broken taillight. Officer B, however, stopped the vehicle because he noticed the driver was black. Officer B is suspicious of blacks and used the violation as a pretext to further investigate the driver. In this example, Officer A's actions were beyond reproach. Officer B, however, was engaging in illegal racial profiling.

Though the data from these stops would be identical, they would fail to capture whether racial profiling occurred in either instance. In other words, no study will reveal the mindset of the officers at the time the stops were initiated. Absent this critical component, any attempt to use data to draw conclusions as to whether racial profiling is occurring remains elusive.

Data collection must be done correctly to be effective. Perhaps the better choice is to maximize training and resources at the front end of the system to reveal why this practice occurs and how officers can better manage the internal fear we all possess: the fear of those who are different from ourselves.

> *"In both cases—terrorism profiling and affirmative action—race or ethnicity is used as a proxy for other characteristics in order to help overcome the problem of imperfect information."*

How Affirmative Action Is Like Racial Profiling

Ilya Somin

In the following viewpoint, Ilya Somin argues that affirmative action and racial profiling are, for all practical purposes, virtually indistinguishable. He questions why conservative and liberal commentators—who generally take opposing positions on the two issues—never reflect on the contradiction of embracing one policy and rejecting the other. Ilya Somin is on the faculty of George Mason University, where his research focuses on constitutional and property law, and is a contributor to the libertarian/ conservative blog The Volokh Conspiracy.

As you read, consider the following questions:

1. According to Somin, in what situations do most conservatives support the use of racial profiling?

Ilya Somin, "Liberals, Conservatives, and the Use of Racial and Ethnic Classifications," *The Volokh Conspiracy*, http://volokh.com, September 11, 2006. Reproduced by permission of the author.

2. The author cites two common defenses of affirmative action in college admissions. What are they?

3. What does the author find most striking about the similarities between affirmative action and racial profiling?

I have long been fascinated by the fact that most conservatives support racial and ethnic profiling for national security and law enforcement purposes, yet are categorically opposed to the use of racial or ethnic classifications for affirmative action. Most liberals, by contrast, take exactly the opposite view. Both ideologies oppose racial and ethnic classifications as a matter of principle in one area, yet defend them on pragmatic grounds in another. Consider, for example . . . [a 2006] *Weekly Standard* [a conservative weekly magazine] article by Philip Terzian defending ethnic profiling in airport security:

> [T]here is no harm in acknowledging that the sort of person who is likely to be a terrorist is not just any citizen who happens to walk into an airport, but someone with specific, comprehensible characteristics of age, national origin, sex, religion, and behavior. So far as we are aware, no jihadist plots have been perpetrated against Americans by little old ladies from Dubuque, but several terrorist attacks—in particular, 9/11—have been carried out by young Muslim men of Middle Eastern origin. No, not all young men, not all Muslims, not all people from the Middle East, are jihadists or potential terrorists. Of course not. But common sense, and the overwhelming preponderance of evidence, should make it obvious to airport security personnel where to concentrate their energies.

Terzian is saying that ethnic profiling of airline passengers is justified because, on average, a young Middle Eastern Muslim male is more likely to be a terrorist than members of other groups. This, despite the fact that not all (or even most) Middle Eastern Muslims are terrorists, and there are of course

How Liberals Created Racial Profiling

It's the left [i.e., liberals] whose cynical abandonment of its own color-blind standard created racial preferences, which are an obvious form of racial profiling. Having marched in the Sixties to establish the principle of color-blindness, the left switched sides in the Seventies to support the principle it had just successfully opposed. Its rationale for embracing the profiling principle in the guise of "affirmative action" was that it was necessary to use racism to combat racism (although it is politically incorrect to express it so bluntly).... This is the most widely embraced Orwellian [i.e., dehumanizing, as depicted by author George Orwell] principle in our culture today. It allows the cynical manipulators of race on the left to smear conservative civil rights activists who oppose race-consciousness and race-privilege as "racists." It allows the left to call itself a "civil rights" movement even while it embraces the very principle that made segregation possible.

David Horowitz, "Freedom from Race,"
FrontPage Magazine, *July 9, 2002. www.frontpagemag.com*

some terrorists ([British-born "shoe bomber"] Richard Reid, Tim McVeigh [who planned and executed the 1995 Oklahoma City bombing], etc.) who belong to other groups. The harm to innocent Middle Eastern Muslims affected by profiling is presumably outweighed by the benefits to national security.

Similarities Between Racial Profiling and Affirmative Action

Defenders of affirmative action, of course, make a very similar argument. On average, an African-American or Hispanic applicant to college is more likely to be a victim of racism and to suffer from the historical legacy of Jim Crow [segregation laws that existed in the South prior to the 1964 Civil Rights Act] and slavery than a white applicant is. Thus, it makes sense to give preference to applicants from these groups, despite the fact that some of the beneficiaries will be people who haven't suffered much from racism, and some of the members of the non-preferred group may themselves be disadvantaged. Defenders of affirmative action also claim that the average black or Hispanic applicant contributes more to campus diversity than the average white one, although there are of course many individual exceptions to this rule. Paraphrasing Terzian, an affirmative action defender could say:

> There is no harm in acknowledging that the sort of person who is likely to be a victim of prejudice is not just any citizen, but someone with specific, comprehensible characteristics of race, national origin, or ethnicity. So far as we are aware, few whites from Dubuque have been systematically victimized by racial prejudice. But numerous African-Americans, Native Americans, and Latinos have. No, not all African-Americans, not all Latinos, not all American Indians, are suffering from the effects of past and present discrimination. Not all will contribute more to diversity than the average white applicant. Of course not. But common sense, and the overwhelming preponderance of evidence, should make it obvious to college admissions officers where to concentrate their energies.

In both cases—terrorism profiling and affirmative action—race or ethnicity is used as a proxy for other characteristics in order to help overcome the problem of imperfect information. If we knew who is a terrorist and who isn't, there would be no argument for security profiling. If we knew each college applicant's degree of victimization by racism or degree of contribution to diversity, the case for racially based affirmative action would be greatly weakened. Since we don't know these things and it would be difficult or impossible to find out, race or ethnicity are used as a crude proxy for them.

Ignoring the Similarities

Some of the disagreement between liberals and conservatives may be due to a difference of opinion on the relative efficacy of the two policies. For example, liberals may think that racially based affirmative action is effective in achieving its goals, while terrorism profiling is not; conservatives may think the opposite. However, this does not account for the large number of conservatives who oppose affirmative action because they think it is intrinsically wrong, regardless of its effectiveness. And ditto for the large number of liberals who oppose ethnic profiling for national security purposes irrespective of how effective it might be. There are several possible ways to distinguish between security profiling and affirmative action. What is striking to me, however, is that most liberals and conservatives seem to completely ignore the potential contradiction between their thinking on these two issues.

| "Liberals are defending discrimination
| when it's done for the sake of helping
| society's most disadvantaged groups."

Affirmative Action Is Not Racial Profiling

Austin Cline

In the following viewpoint, Austin Cline argues that, despite their similar reliance on visible race, racial profiling and affirmative action are fundamentally different. First, he points out that they differ in the motivations that form the basis of each policy. Second, in terms of achieving the desired goal, he claims affirmative action is more efficient than racial profiling. Austin Cline lectures on religion, religious violence, science, and skepticism from the perspective of secular humanism, a philosophy based on reason rather than religion. He is a regional director for the Council for Secular Humanism.

As you read, consider the following questions:

1. Cline begins his argument by pointing out that racial discrimination has traditionally been a product of what?

2. What is a common criticism of both affirmative action and racial profiling, according to Cline?

Austin Cline, "Is Racial Discrimination Always Wrong? Affirmative Action vs. Terrorism," *About.com*, http://atheism.about.com, January 29, 2006. Reproduced by permission.

3. What does Cline cite as the key difference between terrorism and systemic racial disadvantage that makes affirmative action more effective than racial profiling?

The general social, political, and religious attitude towards racial discrimination in America is that it is essentially and necessarily wrong. Given that racial discrimination has traditionally been the product of racist animus [ill will], this is an understandable conclusion—but is it possible to discriminate without animus and for justified, reasonable goals? Yes, probably.

Justifiable Racial Discrimination

In issue 32 of *The Philosophers' Magazine*, Simon Clarke writes:

> Suppose there is a threat of terrorism by a group of people predominantly made up of those of a certain ethnic origin. The government decides to detain and interrogate people of this race entering the country with more vigour than it does other people. This is discrimination on the basis of race. Yet surely it is not wrong, so long as the threat is real and significant. Some governments are currently implementing similar policies.

> It is interesting to note that those who protest against these policies do *not* say that such policies are racial discrimination and racial discrimination is always wrong. Instead they argue that the seriousness of the threat does not warrant the racial discrimination. But this line of protest implicitly accepts that if the threat were real and significant, then the discrimination would be justified.

> If we were 100% sure that a particular threat would be carried out unless we did something, and that the action threatened would kill thousands, perhaps millions of people, and that the only way of stopping it were to interrogate all members of a certain ethnicity (while respecting human rights) coming into the country more than others, then this seems a case where racial discrimination would be justified.

U.S. Culture Continues to Hold Blacks Back

The black-white [I.Q.] gap, [intelligence researcher James Flynn] pointed out, differs dramatically by age. He noted that the tests we have for measuring the cognitive functioning of infants, though admittedly crude, show the races to be almost the same. By age four, the average black I.Q. is 95.4—only four and a half points behind the average white I.Q. Then the real gap emerges: from age four through twenty-four, blacks lose six-tenths of a point a year, until their scores settle at 83.4.

That steady decline, Flynn said, did not resemble the usual pattern of genetic influence. Instead, it was exactly what you would expect, given the disparate cognitive environments that whites and blacks encounter as they grow older. Black children are more likely to be raised in single-parent homes than are white children—and single-parent homes are less cognitively complex than two-parent homes. The average I.Q. of first-grade students in schools that blacks attend is 95, which means that "kids who want to be above average don't have to aim as high." . . .

Flynn then talked about . . . studies of adoption and mixed-race children—and that evidence didn't fit a genetic model, either. If I.Q. is innate, . . . it shouldn't make much of a difference where a mixed-race child is born. But . . . it does: the children fathered by black American G.I.s in postwar Germany and brought up by their German mothers have the same I.Q.s as the children of white American G.I.s and German mothers. The difference . . . was not the fact of the children's blackness. . . . It was the fact of their *Germanness*—of their being brought up in a different culture, under different circumstances.

Malcolm Gladwell, The New Yorker, *December 17, 2007.*

Simon Clarke makes a worthwhile point here. Obviously terrorist groups are intelligent and will change tactics to avoid the likely detection described here, which in turn means that in the long run this tactic will be counter-productive if we focus on in too much. In theory, however, the point is sound: discrimination need not be based upon animus and may, in such cases, be justified.

Benevolent Racial Discrimination

What's interesting about this is what it reveals about liberals and conservatives when we contrast the situation with affirmative action. A common criticism of affirmative action is that it is a form of racial discrimination and, therefore, is necessarily wrong. The conservatives who make this argument would not likely say the same about the above scenario, though. Liberals, on the other hand, defend the discrimination of affirmative action as necessary, but would likely object to the above on the grounds that it is discriminatory.

It sounds like both are hypocrites, and perhaps to a degree they are—but not to the same degree. In this context, we find conservatives defending discrimination when it's done for the sake of security, but objecting to it when it's done for the sake of helping racial minorities who continue to suffer from the ill effects of segregation and racism. Liberals are defending discrimination when it's done for the sake of helping society's most disadvantaged groups, but objecting when used for the sake of hypothetical security (we can dismiss Clarke's "100% certain scenario" as little more than a thought experiment and not something that can justify real-world policies).

Taking into account the fact the effects of social, racial disadvantage is not "intelligent" and won't "change tactics" in response to affirmative action—something which terrorists *will* do in response to racial profiling—and it doesn't seem reasonable to think that the hypocrisy on both sides is entirely equal.

Nevertheless, both sides *do* need to seriously reconsider their positions in light of this and be able to justify the apparently contradictory positions.

| "Behavioral profiling succeeds precisely because it isn't racial profiling."

Behavioral Profiling Is Not Racial Profiling

Jonathan V. Last

In the following viewpoint, Jonathan V. Last describes the behavioral-pattern recognition program first deployed at Boston's Logan International Airport in 2002, and now used in airports throughout the United States under the name SPOT (Screening Passengers by Observation Technique). Using this method, law enforcement officers identify possible criminals by viewing their body language, listening to speech patterns, and scrutinizing their reactions to simple questions. Although the American Civil Liberties Union has raised concerns that behavioral-pattern recognition is racial profiling by proxy, Last maintains that the program specifically avoids racial profiling. Jonathan V. Last is on-line editor of the conservative opinion magazine The Weekly Standard.

As you read, consider the following questions:

1. Why does the author advise adopting the Israeli model of airport security?

2. What are three of the odd behaviors that the behavior-pattern recognition program trains officers to look for?

3. Why does Rafi Ron mention that Japanese citizens carried out the worst terrorist attack against Israel's Ben Gurion airport?

The [2006] discovery and interception of the London air plots [when British police arrested 24 people for attempting to carry liquid explosives onto U.S.-bound jets] was a reminder that, while our intelligence capabilities have improved since September 11, 2001, our airport-security apparatus remains antiquated. Had the terrorists executed their plan, they would have had a high probability of success. Airport security cannot possibly hope to stop similar terrorist operations in the future unless it changes dramatically.

Improving Airport Security

Two options lie before us. The first and more disruptive course is to take commercial carriers out of the baggage business. Passenger tickets would include travelers and the clothes on their backs—no luggage, no carry-ons. In theory, this would lower ticket prices. Passengers could then use that savings to ship their bags ahead of them. (It's not as crazy as it sounds; some people already use FedEx for their luggage.) Today, it would cost you about $120 to send a 40-pound suitcase from a home in Philadelphia to a hotel in Los Angeles by second-day air. This price would almost certainly fall if luggage shipping became big business.

The second option is more practical, although just as radical: adopting the Israeli model of airport security. The Israelis

Ben Gurion's Security Can't Scale to U.S. Size

We could do worse than emulate our allies in the Middle East. Why can't we, or why don't we, have a system like theirs?

Unfortunately, that's a bit like asking why America's streets can't be as clean as Singapore's. Mostly it's a case of scale. The United States has dozens of mega-terminals, and hundreds more of varying sizes; the nation's top 25 airports each process more than 20 million people a year. Tel Aviv is Israel's sole major airport, handling 9 million passengers annually—about the same as Raleigh-Durham, N.C. The ability to focus on this single, consolidated portal makes the job comparatively simple. There are aspects worth borrowing, for sure, but it's naive to think Israeli protocols can, in whole, be fitted to a nation that is 50 times more populous, and immeasurably more diverse and decentralized.

The same applies when talking about El Al, the Israeli national airline. No carrier has taken more care to protect its fleet against sabotage, it's true. Among other measures, every El Al jet is outfitted with an anti-missile system. Crews are trained in hand-to-hand combat, and a minimum of six armed marshals ride aboard every El Al flight. But in addition to being one-third owned and founded by the state, El Al is a relatively tiny airline. It operates fewer than 40 aircraft, all hubbed from a single city, and transports just over 3 million passengers yearly. Compare that with American, United or Delta, just to name three, each with more than 500 planes. American Airlines carries roughly 1.7 million passengers every week.

Patrick Smith, "Ask the Pilot: Should America Emulate Israel's Crack Air Security?," Salon.com, June 9, 2006. www.salon.com

are generally regarded as having the safest air travel in the world because, instead of searching for weapons, they use profiling to search for terrorists.

It isn't as controversial as it sounds. We're talking behavioral profiling here, not racial profiling. Israeli-style profiling first came to the United States after September 11 [2001], when Boston's Logan International Airport hired Rafi Ron as a security consultant. Before joining New Age Security Solutions, Ron had been director of security at Tel Aviv's Ben Gurion airport, which has now gone more than 30 years without a serious terrorist incident.

There are differences between Israel and America. Ben Gurion, for instance, handles 6 million to 10 million passengers per year. Logan handles 25 million to 30 million. And the United States has more than 400 commercial airports. But despite the difference in scale, the principles of the Israeli program translate surprisingly well.

Monitoring Suspicious Behavior

"Terrorists are far from being perfect. They are people, they are human beings, just like us, and they do make a lot of mistakes," Ron recently told NPR [National Public Radio]. The system Ron brought to Logan identifies terrorists by focusing on their behavior. As he explained to *U.S. News & World Report*, "Passengers with illegitimate, violent agendas don't act normally."

Take, for example, the 9/11 hijackers. As Transportation Security Administration analyst Carl Maccario told *USA Today*, when you watch the tape of the three 9/11 hijackers going through the Dulles [airport] security lines, you notice that none of them makes eye contact with security personnel. "They all looked away," says Maccario, "and had their heads down."

In 2002, Ron helped Logan institute the "behavior-pattern recognition" program, or BPR. Uniformed and plainclothes security forces look for behavior that is odd or out of the ordinary. They look for profuse sweat, stiff torsos, clenched fists, quavering Adam's apples, fidgeting, avoidance of authorities, and other markers. When an individual raises suspicion, he or she is approached for what is called a "targeted conversation."

Using "Targeted Conversation" Not Interrogation

The targeted conversation is a series of friendly questions designed to set the passenger at ease, or the terrorist off-guard. An interviewer at Logan might ask, "What did you see in Boston?"—and then follow up by asking, "Oh, you've been sightseeing. What did you like best?" Questions are progressive in order to verify answers. At the end of the interview, the agent either wishes passengers a good trip and sends them on their way, or initiates additional scrutiny.

These are not interrogations. As Ron explained recently, "We believe that 99.9999 percent of the people that will be approached would probably end up as legitimate people, and they are not terrorists at the end of the day. So, first of all, they have to be treated respectfully and not like criminals. Secondly, we strongly believe that treating them in a friendly manner will also be very important in recruiting their cooperation, and their cooperation is critical for the success of the process."

Targeted conversations work. In 1986, Anne-Marie Murphy, a pregnant, 32-year-old Irish lass, was on her way to board a London flight to Israel, where she was to marry her Arab fiance. After passing through several security checks, she was stopped for a targeted conversation by Israeli security because she stuck out: Pregnant women do not often travel long distances alone. Authorities became more interested in her because of the evasive answers she gave. Turns out, she had a bomb in her carry-on bag.

In 1999, the Millennium Bomber, Ahmed Ressam, was caught because of evasive answers he gave to a Customs official at a Washington state port. According to the journal *Homeland Security*, targeted conversations at Logan International have resulted in dozens of arrests of criminals, who exhibit many of the same behavioral tics as terrorists.

Behavioral Profiling Is Not Racial Profiling

Naturally, the ACLU [American Civil Liberties Union] has its Pavlovian response, filing a lawsuit against Logan, which charges that BPR is unconstitutional because it necessarily involves racial and ethnic profiling.

But this fear-mongering misses the point exactly. As Ron explained to the journal *Transportation Security*: "Speaking from a security point of view, it would be professionally stupid to divert attention from non-Arab people. For example, the worst attack on Ben Gurion was carried out by Japanese in 1972. If we focus on ethnic groups, we will miss what the enemy already understands: Using a non-Arab person to carry out an attack might succeed." Behavioral profiling succeeds precisely because it isn't racial profiling.

The success of the BPR pilot program at Logan prompted the TSA [Transportation Security Administration] to adopt it under the moniker SPOT (Screening Passengers by Observation Technique), and it is now in effect at a dozen American airports. In the coming months, TSA will seek to expand it greatly. Despite carping from the expected quarters, they should.

Our safety depends upon it.

| *"There is a significant prospect this se-*
curity method is going to be applied in
a discriminatory manner."

Behavioral Profiling Can Be Just as Discriminatory as Racial Profiling

Eric Lipton

In the following viewpoint, Eric Lipton discusses the many concerns surrounding the use of behavioral profiling in U.S. airports. The SPOT (Screening Passengers by Observation Technique) program has generated countless complaints by travelers singled out for further scrutiny and at least one racial profiling lawsuit. The author points out that leading experts have questions about the manner in which these techniques have been implemented in SPOT. Ultimately, Lipton argues, this brings the effectiveness and wisdom of the SPOT program into question. Eric Lipton is a reporter for the New York Times.

As you read, consider the following questions:

1. Of the seven million travelers who passed through Dulles International Airport in a nine-month period cited by the author, how many were referred for addi-

tional screening, how many of those were turned over to police, and how many ultimately faced charges or other law enforcement follow-up?

2. What aspect of the behavioral profiling program used in U.S. airports worries security expert Rafi Ron?

3. What is American Civil Liberties Union lawyer John Reinstein's specific criticism of behavioral profiling?

As the man approached the airport security checkpoint here on Wednesday, he kept picking up and putting down his backpack, touching his fingers to his chin, rubbing some object in his hands and finally reaching for his pack of cigarettes, even though smoking was not allowed.

Two Transportation Security Administration [TSA] officers stood nearby, nearly motionless and silent, gazing straight at him. Then, with a nod, they moved in, chatting briefly with the man, and then swiftly pulled him aside for an intense search.

Another airline passenger had just made the acquaintance of the transportation agency's "behavior detection officers."

Taking a page from Israeli airport security, the transportation agency has been experimenting with this new squad, whose members do not look for bombs, guns or knives. Instead, the assignment is to find anyone with evil intent.

So far, these specially trained officers are working in only about a dozen airports nationwide, including Dulles International Airport here outside Washington, [D.C.,] and they represent just a tiny percentage of the transportation agency's 43,000 screeners.

But after the reported liquid bomb plot in Britain, agency officials say they want to have hundreds of behavior detection officers trained by the end of next year and deployed at most of the nation's biggest airports.

"The observation of human behavior is probably the hardest thing to defeat," said Waverly Cousin, a former police officer and checkpoint screener who is now the supervisor of the behavior detection unit at Dulles. "You just don't know what I am going to see."

Even in its infancy, the program has elicited some protests.

At one airport, passengers singled out solely because of their behavior have at times been threatened with detention if they did not cooperate, raising constitutional issues that are already being argued in court. Some civil liberties experts said that the program, if not run properly, could turn into another version of racial profiling.

Other concerns were raised this week by two of the foremost proponents of the techniques, a former Israeli security official and a behavioral psychologist who developed the system of observing involuntarily muscular reactions to gauge a person's state of mind.

They said in interviews that the agency's approach puts too little emphasis on the follow-up interview and relies on a behavior-scoring system that is not necessarily applicable to airports.

"It may be the best that can be done now, but it is not nearly good enough," said Paul Ekman, a retired psychology professor from the University of California, San Francisco, who specializes in detecting lies and deceit, and has helped the T.S.A. set up its program. "We could do much better, and we should because it could save lives."

Agency officials said they recognize that the program, which they call Screening Passengers by Observation Technique, or SPOT, may not yet be perfect. But they added that they were constantly making adjustments and that they were convinced that it was a valuable addition to their security tool chest.

"There are infinite ways to find things to use as a weapon and infinite ways to hide them," said the director of the T.S.A., Kip Hawley, in an interview this week. "But if you can identify the individual, it is by far the better way to find the threat."

The American version of the airport behavior observation program got its start in Boston, said Thomas G. Robbins, former commander of the Logan International Airport police.

After the Sept. 11 attacks in 2001, he said, state police officers there wondered whether a technique they had long used to try to identify drug couriers at the airport might also work for terrorists. The officers observed travelers facial expressions, body and eye movements, changes in vocal pitch and other indicators of stress or disorientation. If the officers' suspicions were aroused, they began a casual conversation with the person, asking questions like "What did you see in Boston?" followed perhaps by "Oh, you've been sightseeing. What did you like best?"

The questions themselves are not significant, Mr. Robbins said. It is the way the person answers, particularly whether the person shows any sign of trying to conceal the truth.

The Transportation Security Administration, starting last December, decided to try out the approach at about a dozen airports, including Logan. At each airport, it used six officers who had once been routine screeners, had received an extra four days of classroom training in observation and questioning techniques, and had three days of field practice.

T.S.A. officers do not have law enforcement powers, so if they observe someone suspicious, they can chat with the person but cannot conduct a more formal interrogation. That leaves them with the option of requiring the passenger to go through a more intense checkpoint search, as they did with the man at Dulles on Wednesday. Or if the suspicion is serious enough, they call the local police assigned to the airport to take over the inquiry.

In nine months—a period in which about seven million people have flown out of Dulles—several hundred people have been referred for intense screening, and about 50 have

Jury Finds in Favor of Profiled Passenger

"The jury found that . . . [Harvard-educated African American lawyer King] Downing was unlawfully detained by the state police," said Peter B. Krupp, who represented Downing in cooperation with the ACLU of Massachusetts. [Downing had been asked to show identification and documentation and was detained by police at Boston's Logan Airport.] "The jury verdict puts the state police on notice that its programs, including the post-9/11 Passenger Assessment Screening Program, must ensure in the future that voluntary encounters between troopers and members of the traveling public do not become the type of unlawful detention that Mr. Downing experienced."

ACLU, "Jury Finds African American Passenger Was Unlawfully Detained at Logan Airport," December 10, 2007. www.aclu.org

been turned over to the police for follow-up questioning, said John F. Lenihan, the transportation agency's security director at Dulles.

Of those, half a dozen have faced charges or other law enforcement follow-up, he said, because the behavior detection officials succeeded in picking out people who had a reason to be nervous, generally because of immigration matters, outstanding warrants of forged documents.

"It is an extra layer of security that is on top of what we have," Mr. Hawley said of the program.

But Rafi Ron, the former director of security at Ben-Gurion International Airport in Tel Aviv, who was a consultant who helped train the officers at Logan Airport, said that the agency's system, while a welcome improvement to airport security, was still flawed. Most importantly, he said, too few of the passengers pulled aside were more formally questioned as in the Israeli system, and when questioning was done, it was handled by local police officers who might not have had the necessary behavioral analysis skills.

He cited the case of Richard Reid, known as the shoe bomber, who aroused suspicion when he arrived at Charles de Gaulle International Airport outside Paris, but was ultimately allowed to board after the police had questioned him.

"If you don't do the interviews properly, you are missing what is probably the most important and powerful part of the procedure," he said.

Another concern was raised by Mr. Ekman, who developed some of the facial analysis tools that the T.S.A. screeners were being trained to use—for example, fear is manifested by eyebrows raised and drawn together, a raised upper eyelid and lips drawn back toward the ears. He said the point system that the T.S.A. had set up was based on facial reactions that occurred in sit-down interviews, not while people were standing in line at the airport.

"We have no basis other than the seat of our pants to know how many points should be given to any one thing," he said.

The technique has already produced at least one lawsuit, filed in Boston. The state police at Logan Airport there happened to pick out, based on behavior observations, the national coordinator of the American Civil Liberties Union's Campaign Against Racial Profiling.

The coordinator, King Downing, who is black, had just left a flight when he stopped to make a phone call and noticed that a police officer was listening in, the lawsuit says. When the call ended, the officer demanded Mr. Downing's identification, asking again as he approached a taxi and then telling him he would be "going downtown" unless he provided it. Mr. Downing was let go after he showed his identification, but the encounter led to the lawsuit.

"There is a significant prospect this security method is going to be applied in a discriminatory manner," said John Reinstein, an A.C.L.U. lawyer handling Mr. Downing's case. "It introduces into the screening system a number of highly subjective elements left to the discretion of the individual officer."

T.S.A. officials, who were not involved in the incident with Mr. Downing, said they recognized that people at airports were often agitated—they may be late for flights, taking an emergency trip or simply scared of flying.

They said they were committed to ensuring the program was not discriminatory and would be monitoring the work of the SPOT teams to ensure that the officers were acting upon the established indicators and not any racial or ethnic bias.

But they acknowledged that some entirely innocent parties, like the man at Dulles on Wednesday, would probably be pulled aside. That passenger, whom officials would not identify, was allowed to catch his flight after a thorough search.

"It is like throwing a big fishing net over the side of the boat: You catch what you catch," said Carl Maccario, an agency official helping manage the SPOT teams. "But hopefully within that net is a terrorist."

> *"Japan is an extraordinary embarrassment among major developed nations: There is no civil or criminal law to make racial discrimination in Japan illegal."*

Racial Profiling Exists in Countries Other Than the United States

Tony McNicol

In the following viewpoint, Tony McNicol explores what he sees as Japan's chilly disposition toward foreigners and foreign-born citizens. According to McNicol, it is a climate that has grown distinctly less welcoming in the past few years, as Japan has taken to fingerprinting and tracking all non-citizens entering the country, including most long-term foreign residents. Tony McNicol lives in Tokyo and writes for Japan Inc., *a business and technology magazine for non-Japanese readers.*

As you read, consider the following questions:

1. What percentage of people arrested in Japan in 2003 were foreigners? Why does the author find this statistic interesting?

2. What is the loophole in Japan's constitution that has made nationality-based discrimination possible in Japan?

3. Why was Debito Aruhido denied access to hot-spring baths near his home?

Racial profiling is old news in Japan, which makes us wonder how will a country that so desperately needs immigrant labor adapt to a sudden influx of foreign faces?

Foreigner Profiling in Japan

I tend to avoid cycling past the police-box [a mini-station, known as a "koban"] around the corner from my apartment these days. Not that I've broken any laws recently, but at about the same time I started researching this article about racial discrimination. I was flagged down by a policeman outside my local koban. He asked me a few perfunctory questions, and I politely reminded him that this was the second time I'd been stopped at exactly the same place.

He let me go, sheepishly muttering something about preventing crime. But why, I wondered, should the police be so interested in me or my battered shopping bicycle?

I doubt I'm the only foreign resident to wonder whether their passport or the color of their skin now automatically marks them out as a potential miscreant. Tokyo Governor Shintaro Ishihara has been quick to pin the blame on foreigners, particularly illegal immigrants and foreign students. In a speech last year [in 2003], he argued that foreign criminals were taking advantage of "our low level of caution and lenient penalties" to target Japan: "a defenseless nation with lucrative opportunities." And this past December [2003], Ishihara's warning grew more specific. "While foreigners are not the only factor behind the deterioration in Tokyo's security," he told the *Japan Times*, "they have introduced new kinds of crimes to Japan."

For people like Ishihara, immigration and internationalization seem to equal more crime. Last year's police white paper [report] kicks off with a 30-page section referring to the "foreign nationals who have entered our country [and] are forming criminal gangs here possibly linking up with domestic organized crime groups and crime syndicates based abroad."

Despite Media Claims, Few Crimes Are Committed by Foreigners

Crime has been increasing in Japan for seven years in the wake of the economic downturn. According to the National Police Agency's white paper in 2003, more than 2,850,000 crimes were committed in the preceding year, the highest number since the Pacific War [World War II]. Arrest rates have slumped from 60 percent in the 80s to barely 20 percent now.

Crime committed by foreigners may be increasing—but so is the overall number of foreigners. 27,258 arrests of foreigners (not including visa violations, which only foreigners can commit) were recorded in 2003. That's only about 4 percent of the total number of arrests in Japan. Critics of government policy and media coverage say that foreigner-related crime figures are rarely compared with Japanese crime figures, and that they mislead the public by stigmatizing non-Japanese.

The police certainly aren't hesitant to ask for money for various schemes to combat foreigner crime. [Japan's] National Research Institute of Police Science [NRIPS] is trying to develop a DNA test to identify the race of criminal suspects who leave DNA at crime scenes. According to a summary on the NRIPS website, the purpose of the ongoing four-year study is to deal with "the increasing number of brutal crimes committed by foreigners which is accompanying economic and social internationalization in our country."

Foreign students living in Tokyo recently received fliers from a Kyoto-based work recruitment company looking for

"Spot the Suicide Bomber," cartoon by Glenn Foden, www.CartoonStock.com.

non-Japanese, Chinese or Korean volunteers to go to an un-named laboratory in Roppongi to have their palms scanned for "security research development."

"I was suspicious because they didn't include any information about what the data would be used for," says Australian student Rocco Weglarz. "Maybe the palm readers on the streets here are paying for the research." he jokes. When contacted by *Japan Inc*, the recruitment company refused to disclose the name of the security company or the purpose of its research.

Japan Needs Foreign Workers

In fact, despite anxiety about internationalization and an invasion of foreign gangsters, economic necessity means that many foreign workers have already got their feet in Japan's doors. Some economists predict that Japan will have to invite millions of foreign workers to counter its declining birth rate. A recent study by the World Economic Forum and Watson Wyatt Worldwide estimated that Japan would have to increase current immigration rates by 11 times to make up for its low fertility. If present trends continue, Japan's share of total global output could be halved by 2050.

Advocates of immigration worry that an atmosphere of prejudice and suspicion could discourage workers from coming to Japan. Likewise, Ishihara's pledge to "monitor international students in their study and part-time work activities" is unlikely to help plans to increase the number of foreign students—even as educated Japanese-speaking immigrants are precisely the kind of people the economy will need.

One Tokyo group helping students from Korea, China and elsewhere says that prejudice against foreign students in Japan was rife well before recent scaremongering. Tokyo Alien Eyes, a not-for-profit organization (NPO), surveyed 57 real estate agencies in the city's Kunitachi district and found that 85 percent of them refused to rent to foreign students. The organization's founder Fumio Takano says that students face similar problems when looking for work.

Through a system of paid guarantors, and a work-agency system to match students to jobs, Tokyo Alien Eyes tries to help foreign students live and work in the metropolis. Takano is trying to change the most fundamental domestic prejudices. He shows me a poster telling people to call the police when they see a suspicious person. The poster is in three languages—with Chinese taking up more than half the space.

When police posters warning of "purse-snatching 'bad' foreigners" appeared on subway walls in Tokyo's Nakano Ward, Takano paid a visit to the local constabulary. By December of [2003], the offending posters had been replaced. . . .

Japan's Constitution Permits Nationality-Based Discrimination

The Japan Committee of the International Movement Against All Forms of Discrimination and Racism (IMADR) is pushing for legislation to protect all minorities in Japan from discrimination. Japan signed the [United Nations] International Convention on the Elimination of All Forms of Racial Discrimination in 1995. But Japan is an extraordinary embarrassment among major developed nations: There is no civil or criminal law to make racial discrimination in Japan illegal.

Although the Japanese constitution says that "all the people" are protected from discrimination because of "race, creed, sex, social status or family origin," in practice the Japanese term used for people, *kokumin*, refers exclusively to Japanese nationals. Discrimination against non-Japanese has been explained away on the grounds that it is discrimination based on nationality, not race.

According to the IMADR's Nozomi Bando, a common assumption that all Japanese citizens are the same race allows the government to say that racial discrimination can't exist in Japan—thus there is no need for legislation. . . .

The IMADR also points to discrimination suffered by Japan's one million *zainichi* Korean and Chinese permanent residents. Writing in the IMADR's newsletter, the Association of Korean Human Rights in Japan links intense media coverage of the return of the Japanese abductees from North Korea in 2002 to Korean schoolchildren being harassed on the streets. According to the association, children on their way to Korean schools were identified by their distinctive uniforms and subjected to verbal and even physical attack. The association says that more than 400 incidents of harassment took place—abuses that were rarely reported in the Japanese media.

The IMADR advocates the establishment of an independent body to safeguard human rights in Japan. "A law prohibiting discrimination is absolutely necessary [and] people who have been discriminated against need a body that can confirm and state their case," says Bando. "It's too tough to take everyday cases of discrimination to the courts. It costs too much time and money."

No Legal Recourse for Victims

At present, claims of human rights abuses, including claims of racial discrimination, are handled by the Justice Ministry. The ministry can advise and warn the offenders—but not take legal action. At best, agreement can be reached via the ministry to alter discriminatory action; at worst, say critics, it's just a thin cover for the lack of any real will to deal with racial discrimination.

The ministry is also responsible for the running of Japan's prisons, the subject of frequent human rights abuse allegations. [Human rights advocate organization] Amnesty International's 2003 report on Japan describes notoriously complex and harsh rules, ill-treatment and torture. "The justice ministry would be ultimately responsible [for investigating claims of human rights abuse in its own facilities]. That's the problem. For example, if there was violence against a foreigner in a jail, up till now it was often kept hidden," says the IMADR's Bando.

Despite the difficulties of navigating Japan's time-consuming, opaque and expensive legal system, there have been a number of high-profile human rights court cases in recent years. Finding scant protection under current laws, some non-Japanese and naturalized Japanese have gone to the courts to try to establish legal precedent on racial discrimination.

Two Prominent Profiling Cases

When television journalist Ana Bortz walked into a Hamamatsu jewelry shop in 1998, she was surprised to find herself being quizzed about her nationality. After the owner learned she was Brazilian, she was told that the shop was trying to prevent crime, shown a sign saying "no foreigners" and then shown the door.

One year later, Bortz was awarded 1.5 million [Japanese yen, about $14,000] in damages. The judge ruled that Japan's ratification of the International Convention on All Forms of

Racial Discrimination made the shop owner's actions illegal. Bortz's decision to seek compensation has become an important test case.

Probably the best publicized legal struggle has been that of Debito Aruhido, born in the US as David Aldwinckle and now naturalized as a Japanese citizen. Aruhido teaches at Hokkaido Information University. In 1993, a hot spring near Aruhido's home erected a sign banning all foreigners, after accusing visiting Russian sailors of ignoring bathing etiquette and offending other customers.

At the time, as a non-Japanese, Aruhido had little recourse under Japanese law. But after becoming a Japanese citizen in 2000, he and fellow plaintiffs, German Olaf Karthaus and American Ken Sutherland, took the hot spring owners to court. He also sued the local council for failing to meet its obligations under the [United Nations' antidiscrimination] convention.

Aruhido won compensation from the owners (who are now appealing), but lost his case against the city. With the help of 27 human rights lawyers from Japan's Civil Liberties Union, he is now appealing to the Sapporo High Court.

"If you are contributing to Japanese society, then you should have your rights recognized." Aruhido says, "We are not talking about the right to vote—things that are guaranteed only to citizens. [But to be able] to spend money like anybody else, to enjoy public services that we pay for the same as anybody else."

Japan Resists Internationalization

Jean-Pierre Lehmann is a Professor of International Political Economy at Switzerland's IMD business school. A long-term Japan scholar and observer, he doubts that Japan will embrace multiculturalism any time soon. He calls Japan a "global outlier" as far as progress towards multiculturalism and action against racism goes. "I think most Westerners are totally ignorant of racism in Japan," Lehmann says. "It does not feature in the press, and there is no international campaign."

But even if the government won't legislate to protect minorities, Aruhido points out, the mix of ethnicity that you can find in other multicultural societies is already here. "Are you able to find Chinatowns in Japan? Yes. Are you able to find Koreatowns? In some sections, yes. Are you able to find pockets of different ethnicities? Of course. So I am pushing for legislation to protect the reality of what is already here. Things do change, you just have to keep pushing."

Since winning his case, Aruhido has received hate mail and, at one point, as many as 30 prank calls per day. He welcomes debate and discussion, but says that, surprisingly, "non-Japanese have been the most visceral [critics] of this whole thing. I was asked point blank by a reporter one day: 'Why do you as a foreigner believe it is necessary to do all these things?'"

"I told him: 'I am not a foreigner. I am a Japanese citizen.'"

Fundamentally, Aruhido believes that changing racist attitudes and cultural norms is a resident's obligation: "Anybody who wants to make a place a better place to live has the right, if not the duty, to do something to improve things for everyone."

Periodical Bibliography

The following articles have been selected to supplement the diverse views presented in this chapter.

Amnesty
International USA

"Testimony from Amnesty International USA's Hearings on Racial Profiling," http://www.amnestyusa.org/Other/RP_Racial_Profiling/page.do?id=1106661 &n1=3&n2=850&n3=1532.

Ao

"Yokoso! Fingerprint Please!" *Stippy*, September 15, 2007. http://www.stippy.com/japan.news-and-media/foreigners-landing-in-japan-to-be-fingerprinted.

Applied
Research Center

"Strengthening Racial Profiling Laws: Data Collection and Consent Searches," *Applied Research Center*, March 2007. http://www.arc.org/pdf/case_studies/2007/Profiling_Searches_March 2007.pdf.

Brian Ashcraft

"Hey Japan, Let's Fingerprint Foreigners!" *Kotaku*, November 20, 2007. http://kotaku.com/gaming/night-note/hey-japan-lets-fingerprint-foreigners- 324771.php.

Dirk Olin

"Of Profilers and Public Defenders," *American Lawyer*, October 2004.

Isabel Reynolds

"Japan to Take Fingerprints, Photos of Foreigners," *Reuters*, October 26, 2007.

Julissa Reynoso

"My Name Is Not Julie: When I Least Expected it, Racism Ruined the Party," *Colorlines Magazine*, Winter 2005.

Joel Rubin

"320 Complaints of Racial Profiling and Not One Had Merit, LAPD Says," *Los Angeles Times*, April 30, 2008.

Kai Wright

"If They Are So Scared, How Come We're the Dead Ones?" *The Root*, April 29, 2008. http://www.theroot.com/id/46086.

OPPOSING
VIEWPOINTS®
SERIES

CHAPTER 2

Should Arab Muslims Be Profiled in the War on Terror?

Chapter Preface

Although the nightly news often includes reports of law enforcement infiltrating and taking down domestic terrorist cells, the "war on terror" has thus far produced few notable convictions. Even when terror investigations do result in convictions, these often are for minor offenses, such as using fraudulent documents or committing visa violations. For example, consider the "Detroit sleeper cell": four Arab Muslim men arrested days after the attacks of September 11, 2001, for allegedly plotting an attack on Disneyland. Only two of the four men were ultimately convicted of anything, and both of those convictions were later overturned when it was revealed that the prosecution had concealed important evidence during the trial. One is left to wonder if the suspects' vacation video of Disneyland, fake IDs (not uncommon among immigrants working illegally in the United States), and day-planner doodles would have aroused such suspicion if it were not for their ethnic and religious background.

Another example is Narseal Batiste, a Chicago-born Florida resident accused of leading the Florida-based "Liberty City Seven" in a plot to blow up the Sears Tower in Chicago. As of April 2008, one of the seven had been acquitted, and court proceedings for the remaining six had twice ended in mistrials when juries could not agree as to whether the men were guilty as charged. According to a story in the *Washington Post*, in 2005 Batiste "confided [to an FBI informant], somewhat fantastically, that he wanted to blow up the Sears Tower in Chicago, which would then fall into a nearby prison, freeing Muslim prisoners who would become the core of his Moorish army. With them, he would establish his own country." Renowned security expert Bruce Schneier took issue with this characterization, writing "*Somewhat* fantastically? What would the *Washington Post* consider to be truly fantastic? A plan involving Godzilla? Clearly they have some very high standards. . . . This plot is beyond fantastic, it's delusional." Indeed there are serious questions as to Batiste's mental competence. If he were a street person mumbling on the corner instead of a practicing Muslim talking to an FBI informant, would his name be in headlines today?

The authors of the following viewpoints explore the heightened scrutiny Muslims currently experience in the United States. They discuss whether this profiling is ethical, justified, or effective in protecting America from terrorism.

> *"Historically, in times of national emergencies, profiling becomes a weapon to combat and monitor America's enemies. Now, more than ever, every weapon available must be utilized to combat terrorists who do not value their own lives or the lives of innocent noncombatants."*

Arab Muslims Should Be Profiled by the Government

Sharon R. Reddick

The following viewpoint discusses the position of racial profiling in the aftermath of the September 11, 2001, terrorist attacks. The author places the racial profiling of today within a historical context, citing legislation passed by the U.S. government during World War I and World War II. The author also contends that profiling can be an effective tool used by the government and law enforcement officials in the war on terror. Sharon R. Reddick is a contributing writer for the International Social Science Review, *the journal of the Pi Gamma Mu international honor society for the social sciences.*

Sharon R. Reddick, "Point: The Case for Profiling," *International Social Science Review*, vol. 79, vol. 3–4, Fall–Winter 2004, pp. 154(3). Copyright © 2004 Pi Gamma Mu. Reproduced by permission.

As you read, consider the following questions:

1. According to the viewpoint, how has 9/11 changed the perspective of racial profiling among the American public?

2. How was the term "enemy alien" defined within the Enemy Alien Act of 1798?

3. What is CAPPS II? How does it relate to racial profiling?

On September 11, 2001 ("9/11"), over 3,000 lives were lost in New York City, Washington, D.C., and Somerset County, Pennsylvania, due, in part, to ineffective airport security. Since that horrific day, air travel has become increasingly unpleasant without necessarily being safer. Profiling, based on both the behavior and appearance of airline passengers, provides a vital tool that effectively and efficiently increases airport security.

Opinions About Profiling Have Changed, Post 9/11

Before 9/11, racial profiling was a term that most often referred to a "law enforcement practice of taking the race of a potential suspect into account in deciding whether to initiate investigation of that suspect." Before the tragic events of that day, eighty percent of Americans opposed racial profiling. Today, sixty percent of Americans believe in the necessity of some form of profiling to ensure public safety and national security. The threat of terrorism on American soil perpetrated by fanatic Muslim extremists makes profiling necessary for the security of the United States. Clearly, the U.S. is now engaged in a war against terrorism. Historically, in times of national emergencies, profiling becomes a weapon to combat and monitor America's enemies. Now, more than ever, every weapon available must be utilized to combat terrorists who do not value their own lives or the lives of innocent noncombatants.

Terrorists Fit the Muslim Arab Profile

- In 1988, Pan Am Flight 103 was bombed by:

  (a) Scooby Doo

  (b) The Tooth Fairy

  (c) Butch Cassidy and The Sundance Kid . . .

  (d) Muslim male extremists mostly between the ages of 17 and 40 . . .

- On 9/11/01, four airliners were hijacked and destroyed and thousands of people were killed by:

  (a) Bugs Bunny, Wile Coyote, Daffy Duck, and Elmer Fudd

  (b) The Supreme Court of Florida

  (c) Mr. Bean

  (d) Muslim male extremists mostly between the ages of 17 and 40

- In 2002 the United States fought a war in Afghanistan against:

  (a) Enron

  (b) The Lutheran Church

  (c) The NFL

  (d) Muslim male extremists mostly between the ages of 17 and 40

www.ROPMA.NET The Famous ROPMA.NET Muzzie Terrorism Quiz, *http://www.ropma.net/muzzie_quiz.htm (accessed July 27, 2008)*

The Government Has Used Profiling Throughout History

Throughout its history, the United States has employed some form of profiling to restrict the activities of its enemies. During World War I, the Sedition Act of 1918—an amendment to the Espionage Act enacted a year earlier to outlaw spying and subversive activities by foreign enemies—required "enemy aliens" to register in each state. Pursuant to the Enemy Alien Act of 1798, an enemy alien (or alien enemy) was defined as a person above the age of fourteen, born in a country at war with America, then residing in the United States but not a naturalized citizen. During World War II, the U.S. Supreme Court, in Korematsu v. United States (1944), affirmed Executive Order 9066 authorizing the creation of military areas from which individuals might be excluded to prevent espionage or sabotage. In the opinion of Associate Justice Hugo Black:

> All legal restrictions, which curtail the civil rights of a single racial group, are immediately suspected. That is not to say that such restrictions are unconstitutional. . . . To cast this case into outlines of racial prejudice, without reference to the real military dangers which were present, merely confuses the issue.

These restrictions on the civil rights of German-Americans and Japanese-Americans, respectively, were defensive measures based on wartime exigencies, not national origin or race. Today, while the United States is not at war with any particular Arab nation, the majority of terrorists come from Arab countries, are between the ages of seventeen and forty, and they are Muslim extremists.

Americans Worry Too Much About Political Correctness

The greatest barrier to profiling is the fear that Americans have of offending anyone. To appease civil liberties groups like the American Civil Liberties Union, airport security officials have foregone profiling in favor of random inspections. This system is impractical, frustrating, and ineffective. Random selection allows a young Arabic-looking man to walk through security while a ninety-year-old great-great-grandmother from Arizona is virtually strip-searched. Good manners and respect for everyone will not provide protection against terrorism.

Using Profiling Scientifically

Evidence suggests that the events of 9/11 could have been avoided had the Federal Bureau of Investigation been allowed to continue its line of scientific profiling that led to the arrest of the so-called "twentieth hijacker," Zacarias Moussaoui, a month before 9/11. The science of profiling was developed from the processes of narrowing a list of suspects by identifying areas of interaction of numerous generalizations belonging to all suspects. Profiling, which relies solely on race, ethnicity, religion, or national origin in selecting which individuals to subject to routine or spontaneous investigatory activities, is inappropriate. Probable cause to target a specific individual is different than profiling based on race. Scientific profiling utilizes mathematical probabilities without relying on race as a major factor in the analysis.

Many agencies and businesses use some form of profiling for a variety of reasons. Airlines which operate in the United States rely on CAPPS II (Computer Assisted Passenger Pre-screening, Second Generation), a database system that gathers information gleaned from airline artificial intelligence and other powerful software to analyze passengers' travel reservations, housing information, family ties, credit report information, and other personal data. The CAPPS II system is used to determine whether a passenger is a selectee or non-selectee for heightened security checks. The Federal Aviation Administration insists that, while CAPPS II does not target any group based on race, national origin, or religion, it will be able to greatly reduce the possibility of hijacking. Secretary of Transportation Norman Y. Mineta describes CAPPS II as "the foundation on which all other far more public security measures really depend."

Profiling Is an Effective Tool in the War on Terror

Thus far, one could argue that profiling based on suspicious behavior, not race, has proven to be a more effective method than technology in combating terrorism. Suspicious behavior formed the basis for detaining Ahmed Ressam, an al Qaeda operative, on December 14, 1999, at the U.S.-Canadian border. One hundred pounds of explosives found hidden in Ressam's car was destined to blow up Los Angeles International Airport. Ressam's odd itinerary, nervousness, and uncooperative behavior aroused the suspicions of a U.S. Customs agent. The arrest of Jose Padilla in June 2002 also resulted from profiling. Padilla, an American citizen from Chicago, changed his name to Abdullah Al Amuhajir after joining al Qaeda. He allegedly participated in a plot to detonate a "dirty bomb." Richard Reid, the "shoe-bomber" who tried to blow up an American Airlines flight from Paris to Miami in December 2001, carried a British passport issued just two weeks before the incident. Reid was traveling alone without any checked luggage.

Since it is possible for an Arabic-looking terrorist to disguise his looks or to recruit someone who does not fit the profile, behavior, combined with ethnicity, offers a better determinant as to whether someone is a threat. Airport security agents should look for signs such as a passenger who is carrying a new passport, has very little luggage, buys a one-way ticket, and pays cash for that ticket. Screening every person entering the airport causes delays. By targeting high-risk persons, airport security officials increase the odds of stopping a potential hijacker.

To be sure, profiling, if abused, can be harmful, but it is necessary. Profiling works in terrorism cases, and it effectively relieves some of the public's fear of terrorist attacks. Profiling, when used correctly, is an effective law-enforcement tool and deterrent against further violence. It provides a means of tracking the whereabouts and activities of suspects and can lead to the capture of terrorist plotters before they have committed their acts of violence.

"A world map of countries whose citizens are affected by Special Registration now overlaps almost exactly with the map of Muslim-majority countries, extending from Algeria to Indonesia."

Arab Muslims Should Not Be Profiled by the Government

Mark Engler and Saurav Sarkar

In the following viewpoint, Mark Engler and Saurav Sarkar describe the U.S. Department of Justice's "Special Call-In Registration" program, which requires noncitizen males aged sixteen and older from primarily Muslim countries to "appear for fingerprinting, photographs, and interrogation under oath." The authors argue that this program creates a culture of fear, and encourages Muslims to avoid or leave the United States. Mark Engler and Saurav Sarkar write for The Progressive, *a monthly magazine known for its support of pacifism and civil rights.*

As you read, consider the following questions:

1. What were the first five countries targeted by the "Special Call-In Registration" program?

Mark Engler and Saurav Sarkar, "Ashcroft's Roundup," *The Progressive*, vol. 67, no. 3, March 2003, pp. 24–26. Copyright © 2003 by The Progressive, Inc. Reproduced by permission of *The Progressive*, 409 East Main Street, Madison, WI 53703, www. progressive.org.

2. What are two possible reasons that Armenia was dropped from the list of countries included in the Special Registration program, according to the authors?

3. What percentage of the 24,000 men and boys who came in for voluntary registration do the authors say were ordered to appear for deportation proceedings?

On January 10, [2003], hundreds of brown-skinned men and boys filled Room 310 of 26 Federal Plaza in New York City. The day marked the deadline for the second round of the INS's [Immigration and Naturalization Service] Special Registration program, a new initiative requiring many non-U.S. citizens from selected Muslim countries to appear for fingerprinting, photographs, and interrogation under oath.

The men, who came before the INS of their own accord, had already withstood the winter cold in a line that extended around the block. In Room 310, they waited hours more, not knowing if a violation as minor as not reporting an address change within ten days of moving would cause their lives to be uprooted from the United States.

Immigrants waited in such rooms throughout the country, not as the consequence of any new law debated publicly and voted through Congress but by virtue of a policy imposed by the Department of Justice.

For many people, the price of [former] Attorney General John Ashcroft's policy has been more than just waiting in long lines. Special Registration first made headlines in December [2002], when the INS detained more than 500 men, most of them in Southern California. The vast majority of those detained—an estimated 95 percent, according to some immigration lawyers—had applications for legal permanent residence pending with the INS.

Special Registration Almost Exclusively Targets Muslims

Special Registration, officially known as "Special Call-In Registration," requires tens of thousands of noncitizen men and boys, ages sixteen and older, from twenty-six countries to appear at designated INS offices. The vast majority of required registrants entered the United States on tourist, work, or student visas. Green-card holders, people granted asylum, and several other categories of noncitizens are exempt from the requirement.

The program began in earnest on November 6 [2002], when Ashcroft issued the first federal notice calling for nationals from five Muslim countries—Iran, Iraq, Libya, Syria, and Sudan—to register on or before December 16. The government subsequently announced the second, third, and fourth rounds of the program, with deadlines extending through March.

A world map of countries whose citizens are affected by Special Registration now overlaps almost exactly with the map of Muslim-majority countries, extending from Algeria to Indonesia. The only non-Muslim country included is North Korea.

The government classifies Special Registration as the domestic component of the National Security Entry-Exit Registration System, which tracks noncitizens through airports and other entries into the United States. The Justice Department claims that the Special Registration program has historical precedents that go back to the 1940 Alien Registration Act and the 1952 Immigration and Nationality Act. But its current implementation, particularly the decisions about which countries' citizens or nationals would be called before the INS, relies on post-9/11 rationales.

"With each case, a cost-benefit analysis is made of the number of people that would be asked to come in," says Kris

Kobach, counsel to the Attorney General. "The likelihood of a terrorist or a person who's committed other crimes coming in has to be weighed."

Special Registration Is Useless in Fighting Terrorism

"Terrorists can come from anywhere," responds Sabiha Khan, Southern California spokesperson for the Council on American-Islamic Relations (CAIR). Khan points to current suspects from France, Jamaica, and the United States. Criminals such as [Oklahoma City bomber] Timothy McVeigh also confound Ashcroft's Muslim-only focus.

What's more, the Bush Administration's reasoning seems to rely on the peculiar belief that terrorists and potential terrorists will walk into an INS office simply because they are asked to. "By devoting an incredible amount of resources to Special Registration, the INS may be adding to the size of the haystack, but they're not getting any closer to the dangerous needles," says Jeanne Butterfield, executive director of the American Immigration Lawyers Association. "People are being asked stupid questions, like 'Are you a terrorist?'" She pauses: "Hello!?"

Against accusations of profiling on the basis of religion and ethnicity, the Department of Justice insists that it intends to add a wide range of nationalities to its registration list. However, the government quickly dropped Armenia from the countries named in its third round. That decision partially reflected an aggressive grassroots lobbying campaign by the Armenian National Committee of America, which reports generating 10,000 faxes to the White House within twenty-four hours. But many have suggested that the prompt reversal shows that the Department of Justice never prioritized Armenia, a predominantly Christian country, and included it primarily to blunt domestic criticism.

Not All Terrorists Fit the Muslim Arab Profile

* . . . In 1986, who attempted to smuggle three pounds of explosives onto an El Al jetliner bound from London to Tel Aviv?

  a. Muslim male extremists mostly between the ages of 17 and 40

  b. Michael Smerconish

  c. Bob Mould

  d. A pregnant Irishwoman named Anne Murphy

* In 1962, in the first-ever successful sabotage of a commercial jet, a Continental Airlines 707, was blown up . . . by:

  a. Muslim male extremists mostly between the ages of 17 and 40

  b. Ann Coulter

  c. Henry Rollins

  d. Thomas Doty, a 34-year-old American passenger, as part of an insurance scam

* In 1994, who nearly succeeding in skyjacking a DC-10 and crashing it into the Federal Express Corp. headquarters?

  a. Muslim male extremists mostly between the ages of 17 and 40

  b. Michelle Malkin

  c. Charlie Rose

  d. Auburn Calloway, an off-duty FedEx employee and resident of Memphis, Tenn. . . .

  The answer, in all cases, is D.

Patrick Smith, "Ask the Pilot," Salon.com,
June 16, 2006. www.salon.com

"They keep saying that they will add more non-Muslim countries," says Khan. "We'll see what really happens."

Muslim Immigrants Detained for Minor Visa Violations

Within days of the December 16 detentions, thousands of Iranians and Iranian Americans gathered in Los Angeles for the first of a series of protests and town hall meetings that have taken place across the country. Demonstrators provided the anti-detention movement with the rallying cry, "What's Next? Concentration Camps?" John Tateishi, executive director of the Japanese American Citizens League, says the justification for Special Registration is the same one the government used in 1942. "The current situation isn't all that different" from the one that led to the internment of Japanese Americans during World War II, Tateishi says.

The INS admitted on January 16 to detaining 1,169 people under Special Registration, and to issuing "orders to appear" for deportation proceedings to twice that many—approximately 10 percent of the 24,000 people who came to register by mid-January. Lawsuits and public outrage have prompted the INS to say it will lighten the heavy-handed response of its first round of registration. "It does appear the process was not as smooth as we would have liked it to have been," INS spokesperson Francisco Arcuate told reporters. "If all is in order, they are allowed to go on their merry way."

But despite such assurances, immigrants continue to be harassed and detained for minor visa violations. In January, the INS detained Khurram Ali, twenty-two, an engineering student at Hunter College in New York, for not paying his college fees, according to wire service reports. Another student in Colorado was jailed in late December for being one credit hour short of his visa requirement, having dropped a course earlier in the semester with the college's permission. On January 28, Ejaz Haider, an editor at one of Pakistan's most prominent newspapers and a visiting scholar at the Brookings Institution in Washington, was pulled off a D.C. street by two INS agents and temporarily held at the INS detention center in Alexandria, Virginia, for allegedly missing a deadline to report to the agency.

Damaging the Government's Relationship with American Muslims

Such stories have sparked widespread consternation and fear in affected communities. "In Little Pakistan, on Coney Island Avenue in Brooklyn, the grocery stores, money changers, restaurants, insurance offices, clothing and jewelry stores look deserted," writes the *Pakistan Post*. "It's not just a lack of customers; many of the shop owners themselves have fled to Canada." Says one family head interviewed by the paper, "We never thought we would flee America."

During a recent visit to the neighborhood, we interviewed a man holding a green card. He said he had previously saved $100,000 to put down on a new home in the area. Now, he said, "I am saving it for when I get detained." He added that he and others were worried that after the current targets, the Bush Administration "would come after green-card holders and then citizens." Another woman, a store owner in the neighborhood, argued: "We should register so they can lock us up?"

Given that the INS's increasingly backlogged caseloads already contain detailed information on most people subject to Registration, the value of the data it has brought in appears minimal compared with the program's chilling effect.

"In real honest-to-God police work, where you want to catch bad guys, you better have intelligence coming from the streets—people informing you about what's going on," says law professor David Harris, author of *Profiles in Injustice*. "Like other forms of racial profiling the Registration program is creating the type of distrust that stops people from coming forward to the police with information."

"The government really hurt its relationship with the American Muslim community," says CAIR's Khan. "We're telling the world that we're friendly with Muslims and we want to work with Muslim countries to fight terrorism. But when people are jailed, that sends a much louder message."

Chasing Muslims Away

For Muslim immigrants, Special Registration is a kind of Catch-22 [false dilemma]: They risk possible detention and deportation if they come forward. And they face criminal penalties if they don't.

"If your goal is to make tens of thousands of Muslim males easily deportable, then you may be accomplishing that," says Butterfield. "You don't have to round everyone up and put them in internment camps if you can deport them all or if you can set up policies so onerous that people vote with their feet and stay away."

"As more companies check names, some Arab Americans have changed the way they do business, avoiding transactions like money orders."

Arab Muslims Are Profiled by Businesses

Michael Scherer

In the following viewpoint, Michael Scherer argues that since September 11, 2001, the federal government has increasingly obliged businesses to perform law enforcement functions, checking customers' identities against a variety of lists of "known terrorists." Unfortunately, Scherer says, the low quality of the lists has raised ire and distrust among customers while doing little to increase national security. Michael Scherer writes for Mother Jones *magazine.*

As you read, consider the following questions:

1. What does Scherer say a company is required to do if a customer's name matches one in the database of the U.S. Treasury's Office of Foreign Asset Control?

Michael Scherer, "Business Blacklists: The Bush Administration Is Deputizing Business to Track Terrorists—But Consumers Are Getting Snared," Mother Jones, vol. 28, no. 3, May–June 2003, pp. 17–18. Copyright © 2003 Foundation for National Progress. Reproduced by permission.

2. According to Angela Arboleda, civil rights analyst for the National Council of La Raza, what impact have these "name screening" policies had on Hispanic communities?

3. Why does the author think this program is unlikely to catch many terrorists?

Muhammad Ali's name is a problem. Early this year, the New York-born Muslim went to his local Western Union in Brooklyn to wire $80 for schoolbooks to a friend in Connecticut. Thirty minutes later, Ali received a phone call from the company's offices in Missouri. His order had been blocked, he was informed, because his name had turned up on a government list of known terrorists. Ali, whose name is as common among Muslims as "John Smith" is among Mormons, protested, but to no avail. "They told me I couldn't even get a refund until they got a valid photo ID and proof of my country of birth," Ali recalls, still angry at being singled out. "It was name profiling."

Private Companies Made Agents of the Government

Such profiling has become common since September 11, as the federal government increasingly requires private businesses to do the work of law enforcement. Banks have long faced steep fines and even prison time for those responsible if they do business with anyone on a list of suspected terrorists, money launderers, and narcotraffickers maintained by the U.S. Treasury's Office of Foreign Asset Control (OFAC). But two weeks after the terrorist attacks, President [George W.] Bush issued an executive order extending those sanctions to all businesses, and the administration began adding the names of hundreds of suspected terrorists to the OFAC list. In addition, the USA Patriot Act, passed in October 2001, mandates that financial institutions maintain programs to check every new

57% of American Muslims Experienced Post 9/11 Bias

Nearly 57 percent of American Muslims polled [by CAIR, the Council on American-Islamic Relations], say they have experienced bias or discrimination since the deadly September 11 [2001] attacks and 87 percent say [they] know of a fellow Muslim who experienced discrimination.

"57% of American-Muslim Experienced Post 9/11 Bias," Islamonline.net, August 23, 2002.

customer against OFAC's online database, which now contains 10,000 names and aliases, and federal officials are currently [mid-2003] drafting rules that would require customer screening at casinos, insurance companies, car dealerships, travel agencies, pawnbrokers, and gem dealers. "The fact is, private companies are becoming agents of the government—and they are doing this with almost no guidance," says Khurrum Wahid, a New York attorney representing Ali.

When a company finds a match, it is required to halt all transactions with the customer and turn that person's name over to federal authorities. If OFAC determines that the customer is not the same person as the one on the list, the agency clears the company to proceed. [In 2002] businesses asked the Treasury office to investigate more than 45,000 customers. "There is no question that the number of requests has increased," says Tony Fratto, a department spokesman. "Not only do you have more people checking—you have more names to check."

The computerized dragnet is creating problems for Americans who share names with those on the lists. The OFAC database lists hundreds of common Arab and Hispanic names, often with few other identifying facts about the suspects. Muhammad Ali's name matches those of at least four different terrorist suspects from Egypt and Kenya. In New Jersey, a title company reportedly delayed a real estate deal because the name of the customer—Miguel Lopez—was confused with that of a Cuban banker barred from doing business in the United States. "If you are dealing with more common names, you are going to have all kinds of problems," says Peter Fitzgerald, an expert on government blacklists at Stetson University in Florida. "Your false positives are going to go way up."

Alienating Citizens Without Catching Terrorists

Customers have experienced similar problems with other terrorist watch lists that the government has circulated to businesses since September 11. Mark Deuitch, a North Carolina financier, was briefly denied a rental car at Budget last year based on an FBI list called "Project Lookout" that later proved to be riddled with errors. Larry Musarra, a former Coast Guard helicopter pilot, was stopped nearly a dozen times at airports last year because someone with his name appears on a federal list of suspected terrorists, and Johnnie Thomas, a 70-year-old black grandmother from Montana, was repeatedly detained because she shares a name with a 28-year-old white male whom the FBI had already arrested on murder charges.

As more companies check names some Arab Americans have changed the way they do business avoiding transactions like money orders. "A lot of people have cut back on activities that are not illegal at all," says Mohammed Abdrabboh, an immigration lawyer in Dearborn, Michigan, who had a Western Union transfer of his own delayed because of a mistaken name match.

There is also concern among Hispanics who rely on neighborhood financial services. "It puts business in the shoes of law enforcement," says Angela Arboleda, civil rights analyst for the National Council of La Raza [a Latino civil rights advocacy organization], "and it further alienates the community from getting services—whether it be a pawnshop or Western Union." At least 1,200 pawnbrokers are now screening customers, and the National Pawnbrokers Association recently met with Arboleda. "For us to scare our client base—or even worse, accuse them of being a terrorist—would just be a nightmare," says, Morgan Jones, who heads government relations for the pawnbroker group.

These Measures Are Unlikely to Work

The number of irate customers is likely to increase in the coming months. In February [2003], the Treasury issued a new rule allowing federal authorities to require financial institutions to conduct secret searches of customer lists for suspected terrorists without a court order. "Asking private companies to share information with the government is fraught with peril," says Ed Mierzwinski, a privacy advocate at the U.S. Public Interest Research Group. "These databases are full of mistakes."

They may also prove ineffective. At Western Union, Muhammad Ali was not asked to show identification when he filled out his money order. It seems unlikely that a terrorist in Ali's place would have used his real name—especially since he could have checked the Treasury database online to see if his name was on the blacklist.

> | "The truth is that American society is
> | generally respectful of Muslim needs
> | and concerns."

Arab Muslims Are Not Profiled by Businesses

Daniel Mandel

In the following viewpoint, Daniel Mandel argues that Muslim advocacy groups, such as the Council on American-Islamic Relations, regularly exaggerate anti-Muslim sentiment in the United States. According to Mandel, there is little evidence that U.S. Muslims suffer any notable discrimination, or are targeted by either businesses or private individuals. He further points out that many businesses are uncharacteristically—and, he believes, perhaps unwisely—accommodating of Muslims. Daniel Mandel is the director of the Zionist Organization of America's Center for Middle East Policy and writes about Israel and Jewish history.

As you read, consider the following questions:

1. What are the three examples cited by Mandel of major U.S. media companies being sensitive to Muslim opinion?

2. According to the author, how have businesses ultimately responded to Muslims complaining of workplace discrimination?

3. According to 2004 Federal Bureau of Investigation (FBI) statistics cited by the author, what percentage of religiously motivated hate crimes were committed against Muslims?

Spokesmen for Muslim groups in the West have made a large number and wide variety of claims against the societies in which they live. They speak of racism and discrimination, with the alleged misdeeds they cite ranging from defamation in the media and in Hollywood to physical attacks.

Capitol Hill and the White House seem to think these claims have a basis in fact. After the terrorist attacks of September 11, 2001, the Senate passed a resolution condemning "any acts of violence or discrimination against any Americans, including Arab Americans and American Muslims"; shortly thereafter, George W. Bush warned that intimidation of Muslims "should not and . . . will not stand in America." Presidents and Senates don't make statements of that type without believing that the situation calls for them. But does it?

Few Hate Crimes Are Committed Against Muslims

If America were in the grip of anti-Muslim ferment, we could expect to see a major increase in hate crimes against Muslims and a corresponding lack of receptiveness to Muslim entreaties in the government, the media, and the public. According to a number of Muslim and Arab advocacy organizations, this is precisely what is happening.

The Council on American-Islamic Relations (CAIR), in "Unequal Protection," its civil-rights report for 2005, provides several graphs registering dramatic increases in reported civil-rights and hate crimes cases: 1,522 civil-rights cases in 2004, up from 1,019 in 2003 and 602 in 2002; and 141 "actual and potential" hate crimes in 2004, as against 93 in 2003 and 42 in 2002. The Arab-American Anti-Discrimination Committee (ADC) too, in its 2001–2002 report on hate crimes, alleged 165 violent incidents from January to October of 2002, amounting to a "significant increase over most years in the past decade."

The reality is rather different. Fabricated incidents and frivolous complaints have abounded in these reports and others like them. For example, no fewer than five cases of arson or vandalism of Muslim businesses appear to have been the result of attempted insurance fraud on the part of the businesses' owners. In two cases, CAIR protested on behalf of those alleging hate crimes, Mirza Akram and Amjad Abunar, demanding investigations—and then was struck dumb when each man was charged with arson. Other incidents reported by CAIR cannot be substantiated. There are no police records to back up the alleged explosion of a bomb outside a Houston mosque in July 2004. Another case CAIR cites—a mosque fire in Springfield, Mass.—was eventually ruled to be a juvenile robbery in which the fire was lit to obliterate evidence of a break-in, and was not motivated by anti-Muslim bias. Past ADC reports have referred to egg-pelting incidents against Muslims on a university campus that, on inspection, proved in one case not to have had an obvious hateful motive, and in the other to have been a fabrication by the supposed victim.

Turning to the most serious crime—murder—of eight reported by CAIR in the year following September 11, 2001, all but one had ambiguous motives and on investigation could not be attributed to anti-Muslim motivation. More recently, Daniel Pipes and Sharon Chadha took a microscope to some incidents in CAIR's latest report and concluded that, of "twenty 'anti-Muslim hate crimes' in 2004 that CAIR describes, at least six are invalid." Findings like these fatally compromise the credence that can be paid to CAIR's reports.

"Pope Speaks Against Islam," cartoon by Glenn Foden, www.CartoonStock.com.

Businesses Are Responsive to Muslim Concerns

Beyond citing examples that appear to be outright fabrications, the authors of CAIR's reports show a remarkable ingenuity in defining what constitutes an expression of anti-Muslim bias. Hollywood has been a particular target of Muslim groups for its supposed insensitivity. The ADC decries "the extremely serious problem of negative stereotyping of Arabs and Arab Americans in the entertainment industry." With metronomic regularity, Muslim groups protest action films dealing with Middle Eastern terrorists for reinforcing a supposed culture of intolerance and racism. To Westerners, they present their argument as an appeal for fair play. Elsewhere—particularly in the Middle East—their complaint takes on an anti-Semitic complexion—the culprit now being conscienceless Jewish domination of a Hollywood that slavishly serves the interests of Israel, or of the U.S. military-industrial complex, or whatever variant thereof the subject and occasion demand.

In fact, nothing very sinister is afoot. Hollywood has always dealt in a range of stock characters and situations, and this is not reprehensible when it has a basis in fact. It is not malignity, but reality, that leads filmmakers to depict Nazis as Germans or World War II Japanese generals as imperialists. Likewise, documentaries and films on terrorism that are inspired by actual events tend to tell Middle Eastern, not Scandinavian, stories. If anything, Hollywood has latterly gone to extraordinary lengths to avoid offending Muslims, dragging other groups into service as terrorist villains. In *The Sum of All Fears*, the Middle Eastern terrorists of Tom Clancy's novel were transformed, following CAIR's intercession with the director, into European neo-Nazis. In *The Interpreter*, sub-Saharan Africans replaced the Muslims originally intended as terrorist villains. Recently, Fox acceded to CAIR's concerns over an episode of its series *24* that depicted Muslim terrorists by announcing it would give airtime to CAIR for public-service messages.

Hollywood's pusillanimity [timidity] in the face of criticism from Muslim groups mirrors a sometimes misplaced sensitivity and presumption of guilt displayed by other institutions. CAIR is a Saudi-funded organization whose founder is on record praising suicide bombers and saying he would like the Koran to be the highest authority in America, and whose personnel have been implicated in crimes consistent with these positions. One would expect that, with such a record, CAIR would be shunned. To the contrary, it is courted by government, law-enforcement agencies, civil-liberties groups, and religious bodies. Corporations too have been obsequious, perhaps because commerce is highly sensitive to organizations willing and able to trumpet claims of discrimination and insensitivity. As a result, Arabic-script logos deemed offensive to Muslims have been removed by advertisers; a broadcaster who offended CAIR has been fired; and Internet providers have taken down websites filled with content hostile to Islam—something unlikely to occur in respect of anti-Jewish hate sites.

Muslims Are Remarkably Well Protected

It is something of an Islamist triumph that such a weak case for corrective action has drawn such wide support in a country where Muslims have done exceedingly well. For the truth is that American society is generally respectful of Muslim needs and concerns. Muslim men and women who have lost their jobs for violating employer dress codes (by insisting on beards or traditional garb), or who have suffered even inadvertent discrimination in the workplace, have been either generously compensated or reinstated. Conversely, other groups suffering more from hate crimes tend to get ignored. In 2004, the FBI reported 1,374 crimes motivated by religious bias, of which 954 (67.8 percent) were committed against Jews, but only 156 (12.7 percent) against Muslims. This has not resulted in allegations of an anti-Jewish crime wave in the United States, much less in concerted action to address pervasive racism against Jews.

On any serious index of hate crimes and discrimination against Muslims, Americans are not significantly represented. We should remember this truth next time complaints emerge from CAIR and likeminded groups. In particular, the mainstream media should treat these claims without credulity and independently verify allegations; government and institutions should shun radical pressure groups; and corporations, perhaps the most vulnerable target of campaigns alleging racism and insensitivity, should deploy strategies other than caving in.

> "There is no escaping the unfortunate
> fact that Muslim government employ-
> ees in law enforcement, the military
> and the diplomatic corps need to be
> watched for connections to terrorism."

Profiling Arab Muslims Is Essential to Fighting Terrorism

Daniel Pipes

In the following viewpoint, Daniel Pipes argues that increased scrutiny of Muslims is justified. In his opinion, it is important for authorities to be open about this reality and sensitive to the concerns of the vast majority of Muslims living in the United States, who rightly abhor jihad ("holy war") and jihadists. Daniel Pipes is a political writer and policy analyst who frequently argues that "radical Islam is the problem and moderate Islam the solution." He has written extensively on the Middle East.

As you read, consider the following questions:

1. Why were Ayub Ali Khan and his friend singled out for further scrutiny by authorities, according to the author?

Daniel Pipes, "The Enemy Within [and the Need for Profiling]," *New York Post*, January 24, 2003. Reproduced by permission.

2. Pipes writes that "Islamist terrorists do not appear spontaneously"; so where do they come from?

3. How many of the arrests and convictions listed by Pipes involve al Qaeda?

The day after 9/11, Texas police arrested two Indian Muslim men riding a train and carrying about $5,000 in cash, black hair dye and boxcutters like those used to hijack four planes just one day earlier.

Suspicions Justified

The police held the pair initially on immigration charges (their U.S. visas had expired); when further inquiry turned up credit card fraud, that kept them longer in detention. But law enforcement's real interest, of course, had to do with their possible connections to al Qaeda.

To investigate this matter—and here our information comes from one of the two, Ayub Ali Khan, after he was released—the authorities put them through some pretty rough treatment.

Khan says the interrogation "terrorized" him. He recounts how "Five to six men would pull me in different directions very roughly as they asked rapid-fire questions. . . . Then suddenly they would brutally throw me against the wall." They also asked him political questions: had he, for example, "ever discussed the situation in Palestine with friends?"

Eventually exonerated of connections to terrorism and freed from jail, Khan is—not surprisingly—bitter about his experience, saying that he and his traveling partner were singled out on the basis of profiling. This is self-evidently correct: Had Khan not been a Muslim, the police would have had little interest in him and his boxcutters.

Khan's tribulation brings to attention the single most delicate and agonizing issue in prosecuting the War on Terror. Does singling out Muslims for additional scrutiny serve a purpose? And if so, is it legally and morally acceptable?

Focusing on Muslims Makes Sense

In reply to the first question—yes, enhanced scrutiny of Muslims makes good sense, for several reasons:

- In the course of their assaults on Americans, Islamists—the supporters of militant Islam—have killed nearly 4,000 people since 1979. No other enemy has remotely the same record.

- Islamists are plotting to kill many more Americans, as shown by the more than one-group-a-month arrests of them since 9/11.

- While most Muslims are not Islamists and most Islamists are not terrorists, all Islamist terrorists are Muslims.

- Islamist terrorists do not appear spontaneously, but emerge from a milieu of religious sanction, intellectual justification, financial support and organizational planning.

These circumstances—and this is the unpleasant part—point to the imperative of focusing on Muslims. There is no escaping the unfortunate fact that Muslim government employees in law enforcement, the military and the diplomatic corps need to be watched for connections to terrorism, as do Muslim chaplains in prisons and the armed forces. Muslim visitors and immigrants must undergo additional background checks. Mosques require a scrutiny beyond that applied to churches and temples.

Singling out a class of persons by their religion feels wrong, if not downright un-American, prompting the question: Even if useful, should such scrutiny be permitted?

If Americans want to protect themselves from Islamist terrorism, they must temporarily give higher priority to security concerns than to civil-libertarian sensitivities.

Islamist Terrorists Are Especially Challenging to Catch

In an age of spy satellites, security cameras and an Internet that stores every keystroke, terrorism suspects are using simple, low-tech tricks to cloak their communications. . . .

Across Europe, al Qaeda operatives and sympathizers are avoiding places that they assume are bugged or monitored, such as mosques and Islamic bookshops, counterterrorism experts said. In several cases, suspects have gone back to nature—leaving the cities on camping trips or wilderness expeditions so they can discuss plots without fear of being overheard. . . .

At times, they have displayed a flair for creativity. Defendants convicted last April [2007] in a plot to blow up targets in London with fertilizer bombs communicated via chat rooms on Internet pornography sites in an effort to throw investigators off their trail, according to testimony.

Terrorism suspects are "certainly more careful," said Armando Spataro, the deputy chief public prosecutor in Milan [Italy]. "They know we will intercept their conversations and track their mobile phone traffic."

Craig Whitlock, Washington Post, *January 5, 2008.*

Preventing Islamists from inflicting further damage implies the regrettable step of focusing on Muslims. Not to do so is an invitation to further terrorism.

Politicians Should Be Open and Honest About Profiling Muslims

This solemn reality suggests four thoughts:

First, as Khan's experience shows, Muslims are already subjected to added scrutiny; the time has come for politicians to catch up to reality and formally acknowledge what are now quasi-clandestine practices. Doing so places these issues in the public arena, where they can openly be debated.

Second, because having to focus heightened attention on Muslims is inherently so unpleasant, it needs to be conducted with utmost care and tact, remembering, above all, that seven out of eight Muslims are not Islamists, and fewer still are connected to terrorism.

Third, this is an emergency measure that should end with the War on Terror's end.

Finally, innocent Muslims who must endure added surveillance can console themselves with the knowledge that their security, too, is enhanced by these steps.

The Ends Justify the Means

Following is a partial listing of those arrested in the United States in connection to militant Islamic terrorism:

- *Eagan, Minn. August 2001*: Zacarias Moussaoui, accused of being the intended 20th hijacker on 9/11;

- *Detroit and Dearborn, Mich. September 2001*: Karim Koubriti, Ahmed Hannan, Farouk Ali-Haimoud and Abdel-Ilah Elmardoudi (Abdella), accused of being part of a sleeper operational combat cell for a militant Islamic movement allied with al Qaeda. Specifically, they are accused of trying to cause economic harm to the United States, recruit and train terrorists, set up safe houses and gather intelligence about terror targets;

- *Peoria, Ill. December 2001*: Ali Saleh Kahlah al-Marri, accused of falsely denying his contacts with Mustafa Ahmed al-Hawsawi, one of the 9/11 organizers based in the United Arab Emirates;

- *Ann Arbor, Mich. December 2001*: Rabih Haddad, accused of funneling money to terrorists via the Global Relief Foundation;

- *Northern Virginia and Georgia. March 2002*: 15 warrants executed against several businesses (including MarJac Investments, Mar-Jac Poultry, Reston Investments, SAAR Foundation, Safa Trust and Sterling Management Group); nonprofit organizations (including the Fiqh Council of North America, Graduate School of Islamic and Social Sciences, International Institute of Islamic Thought, International Islamic Relief Organization and Muslim World League), and four homes, all connected to M. Yaqub Mizra, accused of laundering money for al Qaeda or other terrorist groups;

- *Justice, Ill. April 2002*: Enaam Arnaout, accused of funneling money to al Qaeda and other terrorist organizations;

- *New York. April 2002*: Mohammed Yousry, Ahmed Abdel Sattar and Yassir Al-Sirri accused of passing messages between Sheikh Omar Abdel Rahman (serving a life sentence for his part in an attempt to blow up New York City landmarks) and his followers;

- *Chicago. May 2002*: Jose Padilla, accused of being an al Qaeda member who was plotting to release a dirty bomb in a U.S. city;

- *Sunrise, Fla. June 2002*: Adham Hassoum, suspected of organizing al Qaeda operatives in the United States;

- *Detroit. July 2002*: Omar Abdel-Fatah Al- Shishani, accused of smuggling $12 million in bogus cashiers checks into the United States, possibly on behalf of al Qaeda (his name appeared on documents found in Afghanistan);

- *Seattle. July 2002*: James Ujaama, accused of conspiracy to provide material support and resources to al Qaeda;

- *Paterson, N.J. August 2002*: Mohamed Atriss, accused of connections to known terrorists;

- *Lackawanna, N.Y. September 2002*: Yahya Goba, Shafal Mosed, Yasein Taher, Taysal Galab, Mukhtar al-Bakri and Sahim Alwan, accused of providing material support to al Qaeda, and several of them are accused of training in al Qaeda camps. Taysal Galab has confessed;

- *Portland, Ore. September 2002*: Mohamed Kariye, accused of financial links to al Qaeda via the Global Relief Foundation;

- *San Diego. September 2002*: Syed Saadat Ali Faraz, Muhammed Abid Afridi and Ilyas Ali, accused of trading drugs for Stinger anti-aircraft missiles to sell to al Qaeda (and caught in Hong Kong, then extradicted to the United States);

- *San Diego. October 2002*: Syed Shah, Muhammed Apridi and Ilyas Ali, accused of conspiring to distribute illegal drugs and to provide material support and resources to a foreign terrorist organization;

- *Portland, Ore., and Detroit. October 2002*: Jeffrey Battle, Patrice Ford, Ahmed Bilal, Muhammad Bilal, Habis Al Saoub and October Lewis, accused of forming an al Qaeda suspected terrorist cell to levy war against the United States, conspiring to provide material support and resources to al Qaeda and to contribute services to al Qaeda and the Taliban and possessing firearms;

- *Orlando, Fla. November 2002*: Jesse Maali, accused of ties to Middle East groups advocating violence;

- *Buffalo, New York. December 2002*: Mohamed Albanna, Ali Albanna, Ali Elbaneh, accused of operating an illegal money transfer business to Yemen.

There have also been two major arrests connected to rogue states:

- *Richardson, Texas. December 2002*: Five brothers—Ghassan, Bayan, Basman, Hazim and Ihsan Elashi—accused of selling computers and computer parts to Libya and Syria, both designated state sponsors of terrorism;

- *Seattle, Nashville, St. Louis, Dallas, Phoenix and Roanoke, Va. December 2002*: Hussein Al-Shafei, Ali Noor Alsutani, Kaalid Amen, Salam Said Alkhursan, Ali Almarhoun and Malik Almaliki, accused of sending $12 million in cash and goods to Iraq via AlShafei Family Connect Inc. of Seattle.

In addition, there has been at least one conviction:

- *Hollywood, Fla. August 2002*: Imran Mandhai and Shueyb Mossa Jokhan, pleaded guilty of planning to engage in jihad by destroying electrical power stations, Jewish institutions and other targets in southern Florida with the goal of attracting other Islamists, linking up to al Qaeda and creating a state of anarchy. At the appropriate moment, they would issue their demands, which included no help for Israel, freeing all Muslims in U.S. jails and U.S. withdrawal from the Middle East.

| "Searching all Arab males . . . would fail to achieve the whole point of profiling, which is to narrow the number of people to be searched, to winnow the law-abiding from the plane bombers."

Profiling Arab Muslims Is Ineffective in Fighting Terror

Richard Miniter

In the following viewpoint, Richard Miniter argues that attempting to profile Muslims is ineffective in the "war on terror" for several reasons: al Qaeda operatives are not limited to a given race or nationality; racial profiling can be easily evaded; and wide-scale racial profiling is largely unenforceable. He describes an alternative he thinks would work better. Richard Miniter is a journalist and the author of several books, including Losing bin Laden: How Bill Clinton's Failures Unleashed Global Terror *and* Shadow War: The Untold Story of How America Is Winning the War on Terror.

As you read, consider the following questions:

1. According to the author, did the September 11 hijackers display unusual behavior before boarding their flights?

2. According to the U.S. State Department, what percentage of people attending mosques in the United States are of Arab extraction?

3. Women from which predominantly Catholic, long-standing U.S. ally have aided in at least one Islamic terrorist plot?

"Time to get real: Only Muslims commit Islamic terrorism. By definition. Ask Osama bin Laden, who called on Muslims, and Muslims only, to kill Americans wherever they can find us. Yet the New York Police Department has promised that its new policy of subway bag checks will be scrupulously random. This senseless sacrifice to political correctness will waste precious police resources with little improvement in public safety."

—*Heather Mac Donald(1)*

As a contributor to the Manhattan Institute's *City Journal* magazine, Heather Mac Donald devotes a lot of ink to calling for racial profiling of terrorists. In her view, political correctness requires random searches when past experience shows that it is Arab males commit most terror strikes.

She is not alone. Michael A. Smerconish, a *Philadelphia Daily News* columnist and radio talk-show host, recently wrote a book titled *Flying Blind: How Political Correctness Continues to Compromise Airline Safety Post 9/11.*

Mac Donald and Smerconish are making a strictly practical argument. If you strip away moral concerns and constitutional niceties, they say, it makes sense to search the kind of people who are most likely to be terrorists. It might not be pretty, they argue, but it would work.

Actually, it wouldn't. There are four overwhelming reasons why racial profiling would fail: Intent is not a physical characteristic; the category of "Arab male" is too broad to be useful and too narrow to include all known al Qaeda suspects; profiling ignores the most likely al Qaeda countermeasure: recruiting non-Arab, non-male terrorists; and it would quickly become unenforceable.

What Does a Terrorist Look Like?

"We're fighting a war against young Arab male extremists, and yet our government continues to enforce politically correct 'random screening' of airline passengers," Smerconish writes, "instead of targeting those who look like terrorists."(2)

But who looks like a terrorist? Identifying deadly intent is an immensely complicated task.

The Transportation Security Administration (TSA) made a stab at divining deadly intent when it launched Screening of Passengers by Observation Techniques (SPOT) in 2004. "Passengers who flag concerns by exhibiting unusual or anxious behavior will be pointed out to local police, who will then conduct face-to-face interviews to determine whether any threat exists."(3) The September 11 hijackers did not display any unusual or anxious behavior; they had the kind of confidence that extremism imparts. The TSA's SPOT policy would catch only amateurs or the anxious businessman who desperately wants to catch the last flight out to see his son's Little League debut.

Whatever its shortcomings, SPOT at least targets intent, which is the relevant factor, not race. Like racial profiling, however, it drags in too many potential suspects, swamping security officers and clogging the system, making it more likely that a weary screener will wave a terrorist through.

Categorical Errors

An effective screening system would separate the vast majority of ordinary travelers from potential terrorist—without missing a single suicide killer. That is an extremely difficult task, but not, as we will see, an impossible one.

Although Heather Mac Donald seems to recognize the difficulties of basing judgments on personal appearance, she quickly brushes them aside.

> There are, however, no ambiguous physical markers for being a Muslim. So rational Islamic-terror investigators must use a surrogate: apparent national origin. Al Qaeda and other Islamic-terror groups have drawn the vast majority of their members from what [syndicated columnist Charles] Krauthammer calls the "Islamic belt"—the Middle East, Pakistan, and North Africa, where white skin is not indigenous. Does that mean that Islamic-terror investigators are biased against people with darker skin? Of course not. Nor does it mean that antiterror agents should treat every Middle Easterner as a suspect. But they should be allowed to factor in apparent Muslim identity in evaluating whether certain behavior is suspicious. A string of eight Saudi males seeking to purchase large quantifies of fertilizer at a garden supply store outside of Las Vegas should raise more questions than if eight Mormon missionaries were to do so.(4)

As a logistical matter, searching all people who appear to be Muslim will prove to be a daunting task. The U.S. census and the U.S. Immigration and Naturalization Service, by law, do not track citizens by religion, so there is no central database of Muslim Americans. Some 1.8 million Americans of Arab descent are either U.S. citizens or legal residents. Only 24 percent of Arab Americans are Muslim, according to the Arab American Institute.(5) More than one-quarter of people describing themselves "of Arab ancestry" in the 2000 census were from Lebanon,(6) and it is a good bet that a disproportionate number of Lebanese Americans are Christian.

Most American Muslims hail from outside the Arab world; indeed, many are homegrown. Only 25 percent of mosque-goers are of Arab extraction, according to U.S. State Department studies. By contrast, 33 percent are South Asian (from Pakistan, India, Bangladesh, or Afghanistan) and 30 percent are African American.(7)

As for searching Arab males, good luck. The Arab American population is 57 percent male, compared to the national average of 49 percent male. And more males of Arab ancestry were aged twenty to forty-nine (31 percent) than the American average (22 percent).(8) So concentrating on Arab males or young Arabs is not much help if one is trying to narrow the field.

Almost half of the Arab Americans counted in 2000 were native U.S. citizens;(9) they were either born in America or born to American parents abroad. The misconception that most Arabs in the United States are aliens with limited English is provably false, as census reports show. Three-quarters of people with Arab ancestry spoke only English at home or spoke English "very well."(10)

So searching all Arab males or in Mac Donald's phrase, all those from the "Islamic belt," would fail to achieve the whole point of profiling, which is to narrow the number of people to be searched, to winnow the law-abiding from the plane bombers. While Mac Donald and Smerconish's approach would exclude tens of millions of Americans, it would still snare millions in its dragnet. Virtually all of those would be American citizens with no links to terrorism. Racial profiling would not end pointless searches; it would end them only for some white Americans.

New Recruits

If American authorities started detaining Arab men, wouldn't al Qaeda simply recruit others who don't fit the profile? Mac Donald dismisses this argument. "It is unlikely that al Qaeda and other Muslim terror groups have recruited large numbers of Anglo-Europeans to their cause; the vast majority of would-be killers remain al Qaeda's core constituency: disaffected Middle Easterners, South Asians, and North Africans."(11)

Michael Smerconish told syndicated columnist Daniel Pipes that his book-length argument someday might become outdated, "but that day is not today."(12)

Actually, that day is today. Famed French counter-terrorism judge Jean-Louis Bruguière noted in 2003 that "al Qaeda has stepped up its European recruiting efforts and was on the lookout for women and light-skinned converts in particular."(13)

I met with a senior Philippine intelligence official in Manila [capital of the Philippines, a predominantly Catholic island nation in the Pacific] in March 2004. He said he was nervous about the increasing recruitment of Filipina women into al Qaeda. Some were the wives of Arab immigrants; others had worked in hotels or hospitals in the Arab world. "It is a big problem for us," the official said.

Does that mean "Maria," a light-skinned Manila-born woman with Roman Catholic parents, could be working with al Qaeda?

The official didn't know about any particular woman named "Maria" who was linked to al Qaeda, but he said women with Christian names are interestingly common among Muslim converts. Some of them are married to men linked to Islamic terror groups, including the al Qaeda affiliate Abu Sayyaf.

These women would slip right by the racial profiles recommended by Mac Donald and Smerconish. They are light-skinned, female, have Christian names, and come from a non-Muslim region of a predominantly Catholic country that has been a long-standing ally of the United States.

This is far from a hypothetical threat. "Project Bojinka" was a wide-ranging plot to kill Pope John Paul II and explode a number of U.S. planes in mid-air. It began in Manila in 1994 and was headed by the mastermind of the 1993 World Trade Center bombing [which killed six people and injured over a thousand], Ramzi Yousef. Three Filipina women helped the al Qaeda terrorists by opening bank accounts and leasing apartments in their names, not those of the terrorists. Other women seem to have been used to scout locations. If the U.S. began racially profiling all air and rail passengers, is there any doubt that Filipinas could be pressed into service?

Another potential source of recruits would be American-born converts recruited from the nation's prisons. They could be of any color and simply lie about their new faith. In the Algerian civil war in the 1950s, the French gendarmerie soon learned that some of their most devoted Muslim enemies were converts who had found their calling in French jails. There is no reason why history could not repeat itself.

Or consider the July 7, 2005, bombings in central London. None of the four bombers were Arab and almost all had been born in Britain. Racial profiling targeting Arab males would not have derailed the plot that took the lives of fifty-five Britons.

Can It Be Enforced?

This is a question that doesn't seem to interest Mac Donald or Smerconish much. They seem to presume that all laws and regulations will be enforced. But there is always a degree of interpretation. Perhaps Mac Donald and Smerconish have not seen the Somali women in Islamic headscarves screening passengers at Reagan National Airport in Washington, D.C.

Given that 30 percent of all regular attendees in the nation's some 1,200 mosques are African American, a screening policy focused on all "Muslims" would quickly be deemed racist. Lawsuits would follow and the policy would be struck down.

Mac Donald is right that al Qaeda has not recruited "large numbers of Anglo-Europeans," according to the best evidence available. Of course, it takes only a few "Anglo-Europeans" to wreak enormous harm.

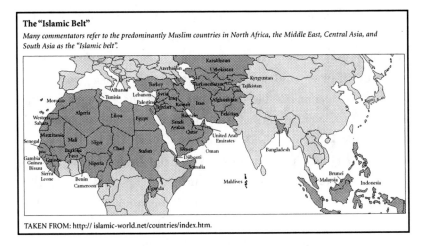

The "Islamic Belt"

Many commentators refer to the predominantly Muslim countries in North Africa, the Middle East, Central Asia, and South Asia as the "Islamic belt".

TAKEN FROM: http:// islamic-world.net/countries/index.htm.

We know that at least four people—one American and three Australians—have joined al Qaeda and have become involved in terror operations against the U.S. or its allies. Let's examine the men who Mac Donald and Smerconish would whisk past airport screeners.

John Walker Lindh. The infamous "American Taliban" commonly regarded as hailing from Marin County, California, Lindh spent his early years in Takoma Park, Maryland, another liberal enclave.

He converted to Islam at the age of sixteen. He traveled to Yemen to learn what he considered pure, Koranic Arabic. He moved on to Pakistan before arriving in Afghanistan. He was recruited by the Harakut-ul-Mujahideen [part of a larger group originally formed to oppose Soviet control of Afghanistan], which intended to train him to kill Indians in Kashmir.

But Lindh was unhappy with Harakut-ul-Mujahideen's lack of martial vigor—a *New Yorker* writer described it as a "fat camp for Arabs"—and gravitated to the Taliban. Since he spoke Arabic—rather than the native languages of the Taliban—he was sent to the al-Farooq camp, an al Qaeda facility in Afghanistan. He saw bin Laden as many as five times and had a small group audience with the arch-terrorist at least twice. Bin Laden even thanked him for coming.

Lindh's case shows how easy it is to penetrate al Qaeda and to train with the world's most notorious terrorist band—and how even white Americans can be seduced into its ranks.

Paul Bremer told the *San Fransisco Chronicle* that Lindh was a "California bubblehead."(14) But only a bigger bubblehead would design American security to avoid searching people like Lindh.

David Hicks. The second-to-last time David Hicks's family heard his voice, he was on the line from Khandahar. As they talked, his stepmother, Beverley Hicks, jotted a note: "David calls from Afghanistan, says he's with the Taliban."(15)

His father, Terry Hicks, took the phone.

"I said, 'I suppose you would have heard what happened in America with the aeroplanes flying into buildings?" It was September 25, 2001.

David Hicks said, "No," and added, "That sounds like propaganda."(16)

His last call to his family was on November 3. He was in Khandahar, selected for a "martyr mission" by the head of al Qaeda's military wing, Mohammed Atef. He was told to guard a Taliban tank at the Kandahar airport.(17)

Roughly a month later, he was captured in the city of Kunduz(18) by the Northern Alliance and ultimately was sent under American guard to Camp X-Ray, Cuba, in January 2002. In mid-air, he wriggled out of his bonds and threatened to kill the troops on board. He was duct-taped into his seat.

Speaking generally of the prisoners held in U.S. custody in Cuba, Air Force general Richard Myers said: "These are people that would chew through hydraulic lines in the back of a C-17 to bring it down."(19)

In Guantanamo Bay, Hicks vowed: "Before I leave here, I am going to kill an American."(20)

Prosecutors charge that Hicks, like Lindh, was trained at the al-Farooq camp in 2001.

They say that Hicks not only met bin Laden, but also complained about the lack of terrorist training manuals in English. He was put to work as a translator.

Australia, unlike the United States, did not prohibit its citizens from serving as mercenaries until 2002. According to the *Sydney Daily Telegraph*, the Australian Security Intelligence Organisation says that at least ten Australians trained in Afghanistan, but remain free because their activities were not illegal at the time.(21)

Jack Roche. With two failed marriages and a drinking problem, Roche discovered radical Islam in an Australian mosque. At first he was a member of an Indonesian Muslim terror group. He was later recruited by regional al Qaeda chief Hambali to go to Afghanistan in 2000. According to the *Australian*, his only exchange with bin Laden was when the archterrorist told him not to go into the married men's section of the al-Farooq training camp. He did, however, meet with September 11 mastermind Khalid Sheikh Mohammed. Roche was given $8,000 and told to lay the groundwork for a plot to kill spectators at the Sydney Olympics, a scheme that was personally cancelled by Abu Bakar Bashir, a key terrorist leader.

Roche blew the $8,000 on high living and tried to tell his story to Australian intelligence. They refused to listen. He then began surveillance of the Israeli embassy in Canberra [capital of Australia]. He also plotted to assassinate an Australian Jewish businessman named Joe Gutnick.

Roche was discovered by Australian police after the [2002] Bali bombings (planned by Roche's contact Hambali) and is currently serving a nine-year sentence.(22) He is exactly the kind of "Anglo-European" that Mac Donald and Smerconish want to speed past the airport screeners.

"Jihad" Jack Thomas. Arrested in November 2004, Thomas attended the al-Farooq training camp in 2001 and was instructed by Khalid Sheikh Mohammed and Abu Bakar Bashir. He's charged with possessing terrorist money and with

having a false passport. According to the *Australian*, John Walker Lindh gave Thomas's name to interrogators. As he has yet to stand trial, details of Thomas's purported crimes are sketchy.(23)

These are only a few of the terrorists who would have escaped Mac Donald and Smerconish's dragnet. If the United States used racial profiling at airports, these potential hijackers would have gone straight onto their planes.

None of this is to say that America's current screening process is ideal. Many of the screening procedures are outdated or pointless. If a little old lady with a walker is going to face down 300 passengers and take over a 747, I would like to see it. Likewise, there is no point in asking whether a traveler has packed his bags himself (the bags will be scanned anyway) or screening for "nervous" passengers (as if harassed business fliers, harried parents, and those who fear flying in any event might not be nervous at the airport).

Currently, buying a one-way ticket or paying cash for one or buying a ticket on the same day as departure are all "red flags" that require searches. This, at best, betrays an outdated sense of terrorist tactics. All of the September 11 hijackers bought round-trip tickets, used SunTrust debit cards to pay online, and made their purchases before the day of travel.

If profiling for race or sex (what Mac Donald and Smerconish recommend) and nervousness (what TSA does) doesn't work, what does?

Here we enter what is surely controversial territory. Yet there is one form of profiling that has a record of success. It is known to the Germans as *rasterfahndung*, which roughly means "category search" or "grid search."

It was first used by West Germany in the 1970s to detect Communist terrorists who had assumed false identities. Using computers, investigators simultaneously combed the databases of banks, utilities, universities, and government agencies for suspects who met a list of criteria. In the 1970s, the technique "successfully tracked down two members of the Red Army Faction [a violent terror sect] by searching utility company records for people who paid their electric bills in cash."(24)

Following the September 11 attacks, German interior minister Otto Schily brought back computer-aided profiling. So far, results have been mixed. Critics charge that the technique has targeted too many suspects (more than 10,000 in one German state alone)(25) and violated the privacy rights of people who have not even been suspected of committing any crime. Schily points to the large number of investigations opened and has refused to back down.

Building on the German experience, it is possible to imagine a more effective, less invasive method of screening people. Instead of asking if a person fits into one suspect category, the system would send up a red flag if he belongs in several simultaneously. Categories based on race or ethnicity need not be used. One category: using the FBI's database of more than 300,000 names of people who have either phoned a known terrorist or been called by one. Another category: has he ever shared a lease or bank account with a known terrorist? And so on. The al Qaeda membership rolls captured in Afghanistan would be used, as would the databases of Arab and European intelligence services. All money transfers, marriage records, and birth records would be included. Add enough data and you end up with a global database of everyone somehow connected to a known terrorist.

The computer could even issue a score to all passengers that would rank their links to terrorists. The many innocent zeros would pass through, as would the ones and twos (say John Walker Lindh's high school classmates). But everyone above, say, five would get a thorough examination.

Would it work? Most likely.

Yet there is little chance it would ever be enacted.

Admiral John Poindexter tried a similar approach with a program called "Total Information Awareness"—and was attacked by the press and stopped by Congress.

That is the real political correctness that endangers air safety—but you won't hear about this from Mac Donald and Smerconish.

[Endnotes]

1. Heather Mac Donald, "Looking the Wrong Way: New York City's New Search Policy is a Waste," National Review Online, July 22,2005.

2. As cited by Daniel Pipes, "What kind of airport profiling," *Jerusalem Post*, October 6, 2004.

3. As cited by Daniel Pipes, "What kind of airport profiling," *Jerusalem Post*, October 6, 2004.

4. Heather Mac Donald, "King Folly: Taking Osama bin Laden at his word is a good place to start in fighting terrorism," National Review Online, August 11, 2005.

5. Bret Stephens and Joseph Rago, "Stars, Stripes, Crescent," *Wall Street Journal*, August 24, 2005.

6. "We the People of Arab Ancestry in the United States," Census 2000 Special Report, issued March 2005.

7. "Muslim Life in America," Office of International Information Programs, U.S. Department of State. See http://usinfo.state.gov.

8. "We the People of Arab Ancestry in the United States."

9. "We the People of Arab Ancestry in the United States."

10. "We the People of Arab Ancestry in the United States."

11. Mac Donald, "Looking the Wrong Way."

12. Pipes. "What kind of airport profiling."

13. Pipes. "What kind of airport profiling."

14. EdwardEpstein,"Lindh in Many Ways Still a Mystery," *San Francisco Chronicle*, October 4, 2002.

15. Richard Leiby, "Taliban from down under," *Washington Post*, March 10, 2002.

16. Richard Leiby, "Taliban from down under," *Washington Post*, March 10,2002.

17. "Branded a traitor and now facing life in jail," *Sydney Daily Telegraph*, Jun e 12, 2004.

18. Phillip Coorey,"Traitor's Choice," *Telegraph* (Sydney), June 12, 2004.

19. Leiby, "Taliban from down under."

20. Josh Lefkowitz and Lorenzo Vidino, "Al Qaeda's new recruits," *Wall Street Journal Europe*, August 28, 2003.

21. "Branded a traitor and now facing life in jail."

22. Cameron Stewart. "Odd Man Out," *Weekend Australian Magazine*, September 25, 2004. Colleen Egan, "The Bizarre Story of Jack Roche," *Sunday Mail* (Australia), June 6, 2004.

23. Padraic Murphy and Martin Chulov, "Taxi Driver becomes Fifth Australian Charged Under Terror Laws," *Australian*, November 19, 2004. Martin Chulov, "Agents Finally Come Calling for Jihad Jack," *Australian*, November 19, 2004.

24. Alisa Roth, "Total Recall: Why the new computer surveillance will probably come up empty," *Boston Globe*, January 26, 2003.

25. Alisa Roth, "Total Recall: Why the new computer surveillance will probably come up empty," *Boston Globe*, January 26, 2003.

Periodical Bibliography

The following articles have been selected to supplement the diverse views presented in this chapter.

Jessica Bennett and Matthew Philips
"Flying While Muslim," *Newsweek*, November 22, 2006.

Juan Cole
"The FBI's Plan to 'Profile' Muslims," *Salon.com*, July 10, 2008. www.salon.com/opinion/feature/2008/07/10/muslim_profiling.

Jumana Farouky
"Profiling the Suspects: Converts to Islam," *Time*, August 11, 2006.

Hasan Ahmed Hujairi
"Hurray for Racial Profiling," *hasanhujairi[dot]com*, October 26, 2007. http://hasanhujairi.com/2007/10/26/hurray-for-racial-profiling.

Carrie Johnson and Walter Pincus
"Few Clear Wins in U.S. Anti-Terror Cases," *Washington Post*, April 21, 2008.

Charles Krauthammer
"Give Grandma a Pass: Politically Correct Screening Won't Catch Jihadists," *Jewish World Review*, July 29, 2005.

Michelle Malkin
"Racial Profiling: A Matter of Survival," *USA Today*, August 16, 2004.

Mary Beth Sheridan
"U.S. Says It Didn't Target Muslims: Mosques Among Sites Monitored for Radiation," *Washington Post*, December 29, 2005.

Patrick Smith
"Ask the Pilot: If Annie Jacobsen Won't Stop Her Fear-Mongering About Terrorists, Then I Won't Stop Exposing the Harm She's Doing to Us All, Either," *Salon.com*, August 6, 2004. http://dir.salon.com/story/tech/col/smith/2004/08/06/askthepilot97_doc/index.html.

Jeff Stein
"FBI Hoped to Follow Falafel Trail to Iranian Terrorists Here," *Congressional Quarterly*, November 2, 2007.

OPPOSING
VIEWPOINTS®
SERIES

CHAPTER 3

Is Racial Profiling Generally Justifiable?

Chapter Preface

In June 2005, the U.S. Food and Drug Administration (FDA) approved a drug called BiDil for treating congestive heart failure in African Americans. This was the first time the agency ever approved a drug on a race-specific basis. Until the 1990s, regardless of the patient's race, congestive heart failure was treated with a drug cocktail consisting of a generic high-blood pressure medicine and isosorbide nitrate, a chemical that helps arteries dilate so that blood can flow through them more freely. This therapy was not terribly effective, but it was better than nothing and was widely used. When a family of drugs called ACE (angiotensin-converting enzyme) inhibitors was discovered in the early 1990s, they quickly proved more effective than the old drug cocktail and took over as the preferred treatment. Unfortunately, it soon became apparent that, for reasons not fully understood, many African Americans responded poorly to ACE inhibitors. This is a long-standing problem in drug research, which, for economic reasons, focuses primarily on adult white males. Women, children, the elderly, and minorities often are overlooked and thus tend to receive less focused care.

But a re-analysis of old drug trials revealed that some African American patients had responded very well to the old drug cocktail. Researchers then developed a specific mix of these old drugs that not only worked well for African American patients, but actually out-performed the ACE inhibitors, generally regarded as superior. Researchers packaged and marketed this new mix of the drugs under the name "BiDil," which the FDA then approved amid great controversy. On the one hand, researchers and doctors cite a growing body of evidence demonstrating that, as the editors of the *New England Journal of Medicine* concluded in 2002, "'race' is biologically meaningless." On the other hand, it remains the case that some diseases primarily afflict people of specific racial groups: sickle-cell anemia strikes one in 500 African Americans but is virtually unheard of among white Americans. Conversely, skin cancers are significantly less common among African Americans than among white Americans.

The race-based approval of BiDil especially divided the medical community. Doctors take an oath to make their patient's welfare their highest priority, and many worry that, by paying too much attention to race, they may jump to conclusions during diagnosis or when choosing the best treatment for a set of symptoms. By the same token, in the wake of the research trajectory that led to BiDil, they worry that by ignoring race (as is increasingly the ideal in the United States) they may inadvertently provide their patients with substandard care. The authors of the following viewpoints explore situations in which racial profiling may be not simply justifiable, but vital to law enforcement, national security, or to an individual's health.

"In the mid 1990s, 53 percent of the people searched on the southern end of the New Jersey Turnpike were black; only 21 percent were white. Discriminatory? Well, consider this: Searches of those black drivers were just as likely to find drugs as searches of the whites. In other words, the intuitions of the police matched up with reality."

Racial Profiling May Be an Effective Law Enforcement Technique

David Frum

In the following viewpoint the author reviews Heather Mac Donald's book about racial profiling, Are Cops Racist? *The author discusses Mac Donald's belief that law enforcement officials should search people based on race, but only in conjunction with other factors. According to the viewpoint, racial profiling, if done appropriately, can play a significant part in reducing crime and contributing to the war on terror. David Frum is a contributing editor to* National Review, *and author of the new book,* The

David Frum, "Support Your Police," *National Review*, vol. 55, no. 6, April 7, 2003, p. 60. Copyright © 2003 by National Review, Inc., 215 Lexington Avenue, New York, NY 10016. Reproduced by permission.

Right Man: The Surprise Presidency of George W. Bush. *The following selection is the author's review of Heather Mac Donald's book about racial profiling,* Are Cops Racist?

As you read, consider the following questions:

1. According to the viewpoint, what else do police look for, aside from race, when searching a car they have stopped?
2. According to Mac Donald, what percentage of the people arrested in New Jersey for drugs and weapons offenses are black? How does this number correlate with the percentage search rate on the New Jersey Turnpike?
3. Why does the author believe anti-profiling "wast[es] time and resources"?

My family recently traveled through a small airport. I breezed through the security checkpoint, but my wife and our 15-month-old baby were pulled over for a more thorough search. As the guard passed the metal detector over the baby's body, another traveler turned to me and said, "I guess they fear that al-Qaeda's recruiting them young these days."

To understand why security screeners are inspecting babies as closely as men, turn to the pages of Heather Mac Donald's new book about racial profiling: *Are Cops Racist?* newly published by Ivan R. Dee.

"Racial Profiling" Is a Hoax

A dozen years ago, some 2,000 New Yorkers lost their lives to criminal homicide in a typical year—the equivalent of a 9/11 every 18 months. By the time he left office, Mayor Rudy Giuliani had reduced that number by nearly two-thirds. Giuliani's anti-crime achievements sparked imitation across the country. And how did the nation's leading newspapers and its governing administration interpret this incredible success? How else but as an outburst of systematic racism?

To listen to the American Civil Liberties Union, the New York Times, and other such voices, American police forces were deliberately and unfairly singling out young minority males on the streets and roads. "Racial profiling," they called it. Law-abiding people were being harassed and even arrested for no offense worse than "driving while black."

The accusation, Mac Donald shows, is a hoax—a hoax made up of two elements, one a complete falsehood, the other a half-truth.

Police in America do not stop motorists or pedestrians for no reason—they almost always have a cause, usually an infraction of some sort. As Mac Donald shows, these stops actually line up pretty exactly with the proportion of infractions committed by minorities. Blacks and Hispanics are much more likely than whites to drive significantly faster than the speed limit and to drive cars with broken tail-lights and other equipment violations. In fact, she claims, there's no evidence at all to support the proposition that a law-abiding black motorist is more likely to be pulled over than a law-abiding white one.

To Law Enforcement Officials, Race Alone Means Nothing

Where the differences do begin to show up is after the stop. Once police have halted a car, they will typically check its passengers for signs of suspicious behavior—whether it is intoxication or carrying drugs or guns. Mac Donald, who holds a degree in English from Yale, is a careful reader of people as well as texts—and she has spent hundreds of hours listening to police. They tell her that race alone means nothing, but race in conjunction with other factors can tell a lot.

"A group of young blacks with North Carolina plates traveling south out of Manhattan's Lincoln Tunnel into New Jersey? Good chance they're carrying weapons and drugs, having just made a big buy in the city."

Numbers Alone Don't Tell The Story

When I was a police officer in Baltimore, probably 90 percent of the drivers I pulled over were black. Did I profile? Race was certainly one factor on my mind. But statistics don't begin to tell the story. In my part of Baltimore, 99 percent of the residents were African-American. I was very suspicious of whites driving slowly around drug corners in the neighborhood at 3 a.m. Some might say I profiled white people. I call it good policing based on professional experience and local knowledge.

Peter Moshos "Driving While Black,"
New York Times, *July 30, 2003. http://www.nytimes.com*

And all those factors put together, police say, can justify a search. In the mid 1990s, 53 percent of the people searched on the southern end of the New Jersey Turnpike were black; only 21 percent were white. Discriminatory? Well, consider this: Searches of those black drivers were just as likely to find drugs as searches of the whites. In other words, the intuitions of the police matched up with reality.

Understand what Mac Donald is saying: not that 50 percent of black drivers get searched for drugs—but that 50 percent of those searched for drugs are black. And this proportion, she argues, reflects actual drug usage in America.

How does she know? Again, consider: Sixty percent of the people arrested in New Jersey for drugs and weapons offenses are black. So are about 60 percent of the killers and victims in drug-induced fatal brawls. In that context, the 53 percent search rate on the New Jersey Turnpike looks like a reasonable response to hard facts.

Anti-Profiling Activity Affects Police Work

Mac Donald charges that the anti-profiling crusade is already hampering police work. New Jersey, Maryland, and California are imposing new rules that will discourage police from using the stop-and-search techniques that did so much to curb crime in the 1990s. And police are keeping score of the number of minorities they search in any given month—and when they reach their quota, they simply cease their law enforcement activities.

Most ominously, though, she warns that anti-profiling may impair the war on terror—by, for example, wasting time and resources on searches like the one conducted on my daughter.

Mac Donald's work is a powerful corrective to the anti-police myth- making of recent years. Let me add just one caveat. Silly as it is to search babies, I myself am not so sure that the practice of random searches at airports is mistaken. In Europe and even in this country, radical Islamist groups and left-wing extremists have succeeded in winning thousands of perfectly respectable-looking people, not just to their antiwar protests, but to their campaigns of "direct action." It's not so incredible to me that one of those wholesome Midwestern college kids recruited to blockade the entrance of a Boeing plant could be persuaded to carry some device aboard a plane. It may be improbable, but wasn't 9/11 improbable? Our enemies in the Terror War are united by their ideas, not the complexion of their skins.

Where Mac Donald is absolutely right is in her insistence that police work should be governed by facts, not wishes. And a good way to start responding to things as they are would be to lay a copy of Heather Mac Donald's important book on the desk of every editorial writer, every academic, and every opportunistic state attorney general who has joined the anti-police chorus. They might learn something—even if it is only to treat with a modicum of respect the officers who risk their lives to protect everyone else's.

| "It's not unusual for terrorist groups to outsource their operations to individuals or groups who don't fit the expected racial or ethnic profile."

Racial Profiling Is Ineffective

Kim Zetter

In the following viewpoint, Kim Zetter examines the overall effectiveness of racial profiling. Citing the research and analysis done by Professor David Harris, University of Toledo College of Law, Zetter concludes that racial profiling is ineffective for three reasons: it alienates the communities that might otherwise provide valuable information to law enforcement; it distracts police from using more reliable methods; and finally, it plays into the hands of some criminals, who specifically choose accomplices that don't fit the profile. Kim Zetter is a journalist whose work appears in the online magazine Salon.com, where this piece was originally published, and many other newspapers and magazines.

Kim Zetter, "Why Racial Profiling Doesn't Work," *Salon.com*, August 22, 2005. This article first appeared in Salon.com, at http://www.salon.com. An online version remains in the Salon archives. Reprinted with permission.

As you read, consider the following questions:

1. Why, according to the author, did terrorists with the Popular Front for the Liberation of Palestine recruit Kozo Okamoto to attack Israel's Ben Gurion airport in 1972?
2. According to David Harris, why was New York City's late-1990s "stop and frisk" campaign ineffective?
3. According to the author, how did profilers working for El Al airline catch Anne-Marie Murphy?

By anyone's standard, Anne-Marie Murphy didn't look like a terrorist threat. In 1986, Murphy was a 32-year-old hotel chambermaid from Dublin, Ireland, who was six months pregnant and on her way to marry her fiancé in Israel. Authorities discovered a bomb in her carry-on bag as she boarded a plane in London on her way to Tel Aviv.

Kozo Okamoto didn't fit the profile of a terrorist, either. In 1972, he and two other Japanese passengers had just arrived in Tel Aviv on a flight from Puerto Rico when they retrieved guns from their checked bags and opened fire in the arrival terminal at Ben Gurion International Airport, killing more than two dozen people and injuring nearly 80.

Nor did Patrick Arguello seem like a state enemy in 1970 before he tried to hijack an Israeli El Al plane flying from Amsterdam, Netherlands, to New York. Arguello, who was killed by Israeli sky marshals as he tried to carry out his attempt, was a Nicaraguan who had attended high school in Los Angeles.

Diverse Enemies

Enemies, Israel has learned, don't always look like the known enemy. Terrorists, both willing and unwilling (such as Murphy, who was unwittingly used by her Palestinian fiancé as a carrier for his bomb), come in many guises, including color, ethnicity and gender.

Racial Profiling Failures

Time and again history has proven that race-based policies do not make us safer. In fact, not only do such practices waste limited resources, they make us less safe. Here are some examples: . . .

The Oklahoma City bombing—After bombing a federal building in Oklahoma City in 1995, the two white male assailants were able to flee while officers reportedly operated on the initial theory that 'Arab terrorists' had committed the attacks. . . .

Washington DC-area Sniper attacks—During the 2002 sniper attacks in the D.C. area, the police were looking for a white man acting alone (the standard profile of a serial killer). Meanwhile, the African-American man and boy who were ultimately accused, tried, and convicted for the crimes were able to pass through multiple roadblocks with the alleged murder weapon in their possession.

Amnesty International USA,
"Questions & Answers on Racial Profiling."
www.amnestyusa.org

Which is why racial profiling (in which authorities target people of certain races or ethnicities) has never worked very well in any environment, including Israel.

That racial profiling can be a tricky tactic is something Americans should understand by observing the diversity of some of the terrorists who have operated on domestic soil or against Americans—Timothy McVeigh (the Oklahoma City bomber), Eric Rudolph (the abortion clinic bomber), Richard Reid (the ponytailed British-Jamaican who tried to bring down an American Airlines jet with his shoe) and the Arab hijackers who crashed into the World Trade Center's twin towers.

Yet [in July 2005] when Mayor Michael Bloomberg announced a program to randomly search New York subway passengers after the [2005] London tube bombings, two city politicians called for racial profiling instead. They insisted that the enemy's face is an easy one to spot and that authorities shouldn't waste time randomly searching, say, Norwegian grandmothers when the real threat comes from Middle Eastern and Asian men.

Loosening Restrictions on Racial Profiling

New York Assemblyman Dov Hikind, a Democrat, plans to introduce a bill that would roll back anti-racial-profiling legislation and allow police to stop whomever they want to stop in their efforts to prevent terrorism. Councilman James Oddo, a Staten Island Republican, promises to introduce a similar resolution in the City Council.

"I thought [Hikind] was courageous to say publicly what many New Yorkers felt privately," Oddo tells [online magazine] *Salon.*

Although Bloomberg denounced the proposals immediately, Oddo says he got e-mails from more than 80 people outside New York who expressed overwhelming support for his proposal. They included a military major serving in Iraq and the relative of a victim killed in the Oklahoma City bombing. But many Manhattanites called him un-American and racist. And Oddo's fellow council members vowed to introduce their own resolution to express support for current laws that prohibit profiling based on race, ethnicity or religion.

Oddo, who voted for the anti-racial-profiling laws, says that he and Hikind aren't calling for racial profiling, a loaded term that conjures up disturbing images. They simply don't want police to fear that if they stop "an inordinate number of people who look a particular way," someone will accuse them of violating the individuals' rights.

"Racial profiling is when you stop people because they look a certain way, without cause, and you're trolling to find trouble," Oddo says. "We never said, 'Stop only Arab [or] Muslim men, and don't stop whites.' We just said, 'If you're going to engage in these searches, do it in a manner that's more efficient and more effective.'"

Being more effective, he explains, means recognizing that the bombings of the Marine barracks in Lebanon [1983], the USS *Cole* in Yemen [2000], and the World Trade Center in New York [1993] all had something in common. "The common denominator is that every jihadi [holy warrior] who is engaged in international terrorism has been a young fundamentalist," Oddo says. "We shouldn't try to couch that reality in some politically correct terms."

Racial Profiling Is Worse Than Ineffective

Some people do consider racial profiling unethical, but there are plenty of other reasons to reject racial profiling, even aside from its violation of equal protection [i.e., 14th Amendment of the U.S. Constitution] rights.

David Harris, professor of law and values at the University of Toledo College of Law in Ohio, says that focusing on specific ethnic groups alienates the very people authorities need to help them catch terrorists. "By the time the threat is at the subway or airport, we're down to the last line of defense," Harris says. "You really want to catch these people before they go to the subway."

That can be accomplished only by gathering information from people who live in the communities where sleeper cells reside and can tell authorities who's new in a neighborhood and who seems to have income without holding a job.

But the most important reason to oppose racial profiling, says Harris, the author of *Profiles in Injustice: Why Racial Profiling Cannot Work* is that, as the title of his book suggests, it simply doesn't work.

Harris says that when police use race or ethnic appearance as a factor in law enforcement, their accuracy in catching criminals decreases. Even worse, it can lead to accidental deaths, such as the fatal shooting by London police of an innocent Brazilian man after the [2005] bombings there.

A Lot of Trouble for a Little Reward

Harris points to a study of New York's "stop and frisk" campaign in the late 1990s, when police were stopping people in the streets on a regular basis in an effort to confiscate illegal weapons and reduce crime. The campaign created tension between the police and minority communities who thought they were being unfairly targeted for frisks. It turned out they were right.

After Amadou Diallo, an unarmed West African immigrant, was killed during a stop, New York attorney general Eliot Spitzer ordered a study of 175,000 "stop and frisk" records and found that although African-Americans composed only 25 percent of New York City's population at the time, they made up 50 percent of the people who were stopped. Latinos were roughly 23 percent of the population and 33 percent of those stopped, while whites were 43 percent of the population and 13 percent of those stopped.

These findings interested Harris less than what the statistics indicated about the results: Police were going to a lot of trouble for little reward especially when the people they stopped were African-Americans.

Focusing on Appearance Instead of Behavior

Harris looked at what he called "hit rates"—the percentage of stops in which the police found drugs, a gun or something else that led to an arrest—noted that the number of hits in general was very low for the number of stops that police made. But more interesting was that the rate for African-

Americans was much lower than the rate for Caucasians. Police had a hit rate of 12.6 percent when they stopped Caucasians and only 10.5 percent when they stopped African-Americans. The hit rate for Latinos was 11.5 percent.

"You might say that we have a difference of 2.1 percent between blacks and whites. But it's actually a difference of 20 percent when you do the math right." Harris says. And "the difference between whites and Latinos is about 10 percent."

Essentially, police were stopping more African-Americans than Caucasians but finding fewer criminals among the former. Why? Not because blacks commit proportionately fewer crimes than whites do (the data vary according to the type of crime and other factors) but because police were looking at the wrong factors when they stopped people, Harris says.

"They're focusing on appearance when they should be focusing on behavior," he says. "When they're not distracted by race, they're actually doing a more accurate job" of picking out the right people.

Focusing on appearance produces a lot of false positives. And "every time you introduce a false positive, you take resources away from your ability to focus on people who are really of interest—those who are behaving suspiciously," Harris says. "If it's a question of finding a needle in a haystack . . . don't put more hay on the top."

Recognizing the Signs

What does work in preventing terrorism, Harris says, is behavior profiling. "If you're going to catch people who mean to put bombs on your subway trains or in airplanes, you don't actually care [if they're] young Muslim men . . . You care about [keeping] anyone from boarding the airplane who is going to behave like a terrorist."

Yuval Bezherano agrees. Bezherano is the executive vice president of New Age Security Solutions [NASS], a company that teaches people how to identify behaviors that indicate a person is concealing something and could be a security risk. The technique is called behavior pattern recognition and is modeled after methods used in Israel. NASS's president, Rafi Ron, is a former security chief at Ben Gurion Airport. The company has trained authorities at Boston's Logan International Airport as well as personnel at the Statue of Liberty. Recently the company trained about 100 employees of New York's subway and bus system.

The signs to watch for can be as obvious as someone acting nervous and sweating profusely on a cold day or as subtle as someone walking awkwardly in a way that indicates the person could be wearing a belt of explosives.

"It's always the unusual, the thing that doesn't fit," Bezherano says. "If you know your environment and what is usual for the environment, you know what to look for."

Depending on the situation, the next step might be to engage the person in a targeted conversation to determine whether he or she should be elevated to a higher level of risk or cleared from consideration.

Terrorists Dodge the Profile

It was this kind of screening that caught Anne-Marie Murphy, who initially raised interest among El Al's security staff because she was a pregnant woman traveling a long distance alone, something that Bezherano says is unusual behavior. She'd already cleared three security checkpoints at London's Heathrow Airport before an El Al "profiler" asked her where she'd be staying in Israel. Murphy's fiancé had warned her not to tell authorities about him because they would interrogate her if they knew she had an Arab boyfriend, so she told the profiler she'd be staying at the Hilton Hotel in Bethlehem. The profiler knew there were only two Hiltons and that neither was in Bethlehem. When authorities searched Murphy's bag, they discovered several pounds of plastic explosives concealed in a false bottom and a microchip detonator hidden in a pocket calculator.

Behavior profiling is much more effective than racial profiling, Bezherano says, because it's not unusual for terrorist groups to outsource their operations to individuals or groups who don't fit the expected racial or ethnic profile.

Patrick Arguello was a member of the [Nicaraguan] Sandinista National Liberation Front when he posed as the husband of a woman who was an operative for the Popular Front for the Liberation of Palestine [PFLP] to help her hijack the El Al plane.

Kozo Okamoto was a member of the Japanese Red Army, which attacked Ben Gurion Airport; the group shared the Marxist ideologies of the PFLP.

Bezherano says there's no reason to believe that al-Qaida won't, or doesn't, farm out some of its tasks to other groups. "The philosophy of terrorist organizations is that the enemy of your enemy is your friend," Bezherano says. "Even though al-Qaida is very extreme, [its members] will collaborate with others as long as it serves its cause."

If those working to prevent terrorist attacks on U.S. soil engage in racial or ethnic profiling, they're merely playing into terrorists' hands—and are likely to miss some of the enemies right in front of their eyes.

> *"It's perfectly reasonable to decide not to implement a countermeasure not because it doesn't work, but because the trade-offs are too great."*

Profiling Can Be Effective but May Be Too Costly

Bruce Schneier

In the following viewpoint, Bruce Schneier contends that profiling—especially when performed by intelligent humans rather than by automated machines—may be an effective security solution, but that the trade-offs inherent in using racial profiling are rarely a good deal. He argues that the most important part of a security system is not the hardware, software, or protocol, but the people implementing it. Bruce Schneier is a noted expert on cryptography and security, and the author of Beyond Fear: Thinking Sensibly About Security in an Uncertain World.

As you read, consider the following questions:

1. What weakness does Schneier see in profiling done by computers instead of humans?

Bruce Schneier, *Beyond Fear: Thinking Sensibly About Security in an Uncertain World*, Heidelberg, New York: Copernicus Books, 2003, pp. 133–137. Copyright © 2003 Bruce Schneier. All rights reserved. Reproduced by permission of the author.

155

2. What did a 1983 commission conclude about the World War II imprisonment of Japanese Americans?

3. According to the author, did U.S. Customs agent Diana Dean use racial profiling to catch would-be plane bomber Ahmed Ressam?

Good security has people in charge. People are resilient. People can improvise. People can be creative. People can develop on-the-spot solutions. People can detect attackers who cheat, and can attempt to maintain security despite the cheating. People can detect passive failures and attempt to recover. People are the strongest point in a security process. When a security system succeeds in the face of a new or coordinated or devastating attack, it's usually due to the efforts of people.

A "Hinky" Terrorist

Here's an example: On 14 December 1999, Ahmed Ressam tried to enter the U.S. by ferryboat from Victoria Island, British Columbia. In the trunk of his car, he had a suitcase bomb. His plan was to drive to Los Angeles International Airport, put his suitcase on a luggage cart in the terminal, set the timer, and then leave. The plan would have worked had someone not been vigilant.

Ressam had to clear customs before boarding the ferry. He had fake ID, in the name of Benni Antoine Noris, and the computer cleared him based on this ID. He was allowed to go through after a routine check of his car's trunk, even though he was wanted by the Canadian police. On the other side of the Strait of Juan de Fuca, at Port Angeles, Washington, Ressam was approached by U.S. customs agent Diana Dean, who asked some routine questions and then decided that he looked suspicious. He was fidgeting, sweaty, and jittery. He avoided eye contact. In Dean's own words, he was acting "hinky." More questioning—there was no one else crossing the border, so two other agents got involved—and more hinky behavior. Ressam's car was eventually searched, and he was finally discovered and captured. It wasn't any one thing that tipped Dean off; it was everything encompassed in the slang term "hinky." But the system worked. The reason there wasn't a bombing at LAX [Los Angeles International Airport] around Christmas in 1999 was because a knowledgeable person was in charge of security and paying attention.

Profiling by People Versus Profiling by Computers

There's a dirty word for what Dean did that chilly afternoon in December, and it's *profiling*. Everyone does it all the time. When you see someone lurking in a dark alley and change your direction to avoid him, you're profiling. When a storeowner sees someone furtively looking around as she fiddles inside her jacket, that storeowner is profiling. People profile based on someone's dress, mannerisms, tone of voice . . . and yes, also on their race and ethnicity. When you see someone running toward you on the street with a bloody ax, you don't know for sure that he's a crazed ax murderer. Perhaps he's a butcher who's actually running after the person next to you to give her the change she forgot. But you're going to make a guess one way or another. That guess is an example of profiling.

To profile is to generalize. It's taking characteristics of a population and applying them to an individual. People naturally have an intuition about other people based on different characteristics. Sometimes that intuition is right and sometimes it's wrong, but it's still a person's first reaction. How good this intuition is as a countermeasure depends on two things: how accurate the intuition is and how effective it is when it becomes institutionalized or when the profile characteristics become commonplace.

One of the ways profiling becomes institutionalized is through computerization. Instead of Diana Dean looking someone over, a computer looks the profile over and gives it some sort of rating. Generally profiles with high ratings are further evaluated by people, although sometimes countermeasures kick in based on the computerized profile alone. This is, of course, more brittle. The computer can profile based only on simple, easy-to-assign characteristics: age, race, credit history, job history, et cetera. Computers don't get hinky feelings. Computers also can't adapt the way people can.

Profiling Must Be Accurate to Work

Profiling works better if the characteristics profiled are accurate. If erratic driving is a good indication that the driver is intoxicated, then that's a good characteristic for a police officer to use to determine who he's going to pull over. If furtively looking around a store or wearing a coat on a hot day is a good indication that the person is a shoplifter, then those are good characteristics for a store owner to pay attention to. But if wearing baggy trousers isn't a good indication that the person is a shoplifter, then the store owner is going to spend a lot of time paying undue attention to honest people with lousy fashion sense.

In common parlance, the term "profiling" doesn't refer to these characteristics. It refers to profiling based on characteristics like race and ethnicity, and *institutionalized* profiling based on those characteristics alone. During World War II, the U.S. rounded up over 100,000 people of Japanese origin who lived on the West Coast and locked them in camps (prisons, really). That was an example of profiling. Israeli border guards spend a lot more time scrutinizing Arab men than Israeli women; that's another example of profiling. In many U.S. communities, police have been known to stop and question people of color driving around in wealthy white neighborhoods (commonly referred to as "DWB"—Driving While Black). In all of these cases you might possibly be able to argue some security benefit, but the trade-offs are enormous: Honest people who fit the profile can get annoyed, or harassed, or arrested, when they're assumed to be attackers.

For democratic governments, this is a major problem. It's just wrong to segregate people into "more likely to be attackers" and "less likely to be attackers" based on race or ethnicity. It's wrong for the police to pull a car over just because its black occupants are driving in a rich white neighborhood. It's discrimination.

Bad Security Trade-Offs

But people make bad security trade-offs when they're scared, which is why we saw Japanese internment camps during World War II, and why there is so much discrimination against Arabs in the U.S. going on today. That doesn't make it right, and it doesn't make it effective security. Writing about the Japanese internment, for example, a 1983 [congressional] commission reported that the causes of the incarceration were rooted in "race prejudice, war hysteria, and a failure of political leadership." But just because something is wrong doesn't mean that people won't continue to do it.

Ethics aside, institutionalized profiling fails because real attackers are so rare: Active failures will be much more common than passive failures. The great majority of people who fit the profile will be innocent. At the same time, some real attackers are going to deliberately try to sneak past the profile. During World War II, a Japanese American saboteur could try to evade imprisonment by pretending to be Chinese. Similarly, an Arab terrorist could dye his hair blond, practice an American accent, and so on.

Profiling can also blind you to threats outside the profile. If U.S. border guards stop and search everyone who's young, Arab, and male, they're not going to have the time to stop and search all sorts of other people, no matter how hinky they might be acting. On the other hand, if the attackers are of a single race or ethnicity, profiling is more likely to work (although the ethics are still questionable). It makes real security sense for [Israeli airline] El Al to spend more time investigating young Arab males than it does for them to investigate Israeli families. In Vietnam, American soldiers never knew which local civilians were really combatants; sometimes killing all of them was the security solution they chose.

If a lot of this discussion is abhorrent, as it probably should be, it's the trade-offs in your head talking. It's perfectly reasonable to decide not to implement a countermeasure not because it doesn't work, but because the trade-offs are too great. Locking up every Arab-looking person will reduce the potential for Muslim terrorism, but no reasonable person would suggest it. (It's an example of "winning the battle but losing the war.") In the U.S., there are laws that prohibit police profiling by characteristics like ethnicity, because we believe that such security measures are wrong (and not simply because we believe them to be ineffective).

Intuition Is Good Security

Still, no matter how much a government makes it illegal, profiling does occur. It occurs at an individual level, at the level of Diana Dean deciding which cars to wave through and which ones to investigate further. She profiled Ressam based on his mannerisms and his answers to her questions. He was Algerian, and she certainly noticed that. However, this was before 9/11, and the reports of the incident clearly indicate that she thought he was a drug smuggler; ethnicity probably wasn't a key profiling factor in this case. In fact, this is one of the most interesting aspects of the story. That intuitive sense that something was amiss worked beautifully, even though everybody made a wrong assumption about *what* was wrong. Human intuition detected a completely unexpected kind of attack. Humans will beat computers at hinkiness-detection for many decades to come.

And done correctly, this intuition-based sort of profiling can be an excellent security countermeasure. Dean needed to have the training and the experience to profile accurately and properly, without stepping over the line and profiling illegally. The trick here is to make sure perceptions of risk match the actual risks. If those responsible for security profile based on superstition and wrong-headed intuition, or by blindly following a computerized profiling system, profiling won't work at all. And even worse, it actually can reduce security by blinding people to the real threats. Institutionalized profiling can ossify [turn into bone] a mind, and a person's mind is the most important security countermeasure we have.

> *"The Haradas were neither radical na-*
> *tionalists nor professional spies. They*
> *were ordinary Japanese-Americans who*
> *betrayed America by putting their eth-*
> *nic roots first."*

Profiling Japanese Americans During World War II Was Necessary

Michelle Malkin

During World War II roughly 110,000 U.S. residents of Japanese descent were forcibly removed from their homes on the West Coast of the United States and held in "war relocation camps." In the following viewpoint, Michelle Malkin argues that the internment of Japanese Americans was necessary, even though the U.S. government acknowledged that fewer than 25 percent had any inclination to be disloyal to the United States. Michelle Malkin is a conservative columnist and blogger, and the author of In Defense of Internment: The Case for "Racial Profiling" in World War II and the War on Terror.

Michelle Malkin, "The Turncoats on Niihau Island," *FrontPage Magazine*, Townhall.com, August 10, 2004. Reproduced by permission of Michelle Malkin and Creators Syndicate.

As you read, consider the following questions:

1. According to the author, why did Howard Kaleohano introduce the captured Japanese pilot to a group of Japanese Americans?
2. According to the author, why did Yoshio and Irene Harada help the captured pilot escape?
3. According to the author, how did President Franklin D. Roosevelt and his administration react to the story of Nishikaichi and the Haradas?

"*Are you a Japanese?*"

Those were the first English words spoken by downed Japanese fighter pilot Shigenori Nishikaichi on tiny Niihau Island, located about one hundred miles northwest of Honolulu. It was December 7, 1941. Nishikaichi had had a busy, bloody morning at Pearl Harbor. Now, with the aid and comfort of a Japanese-American couple, Nishikaichi was about to make the lives of the Niihau residents a living hell.

A Japanese Pilot Crashes

Around 7:00 a.m., Nishikaichi boarded his Zero single-seat fighter plane and took off from the carrier Hiryu in the Pacific. An hour and a half later, the young Japanese pilot strafed planes, trucks, and personnel on Oahu. Headed back to his carrier, Nishikaichi and some fellow pilots encountered a group of American P36 fighter planes. During the air battle, Nishikaichi's plane took several hits. One punctured the Zero's gas tank. Nishikaichi steered the crippled plane toward the westernmost Hawaiian island: Niihau. Fewer than 200 Hawaiians plus three laborers of Japanese descent called Niihau home. Japan planned to use the island as a submarine pickup point for stranded pilots.

Nishikaichi crash-landed the plane in a field near one of the ranch homes. The first to reach him was Hawila "Howard"

Kaleohano, a burly Hawaiian. The island had no telephones. On that tranquil, late Sunday morning, none of the inhabitants was yet aware of the death and destruction that had just rained down on Pearl Harbor.

Nonetheless, Kaleohano wisely confiscated the dazed Nishikaichi's gun and papers. Kaleohano, perhaps the most educated Hawaiian on Niihau, had been keeping tabs on world affairs through newspapers supplied by ranch owner Aylmer Robinson (who paid weekly visits to the island and lived twenty miles away on Kauai). Wary but warm, Kaleohano brought the enemy pilot to his home. Along the way, Nishikaichi asked Kaleohano if he was "a Japanese." The answer was an emphatic "No."

After sharing a meal and cigarettes, Nishikaichi demanded that Kaleohano return his papers, which included maps, radio codes, and Pearl Harbor attack plans. Kaleohano refused. To make their communication easier, Kaleohano asked his neighbors to summon one of the island's three residents of Japanese descent to translate for Nishikaichi. They first brought a Japanese-born immigrant, Ishimatsu Shintani, to the house. He reluctantly exchanged a few words with the pilot in Japanese, but left in a hurry—apparently sensing trouble.

Choosing Ethnic Ties over Neighbors

The islanders then turned to Yoshio Harada and his wife Irene, both U.S. citizens, born in Hawaii to Japanese immigrants. Harada had moved from Kauai to California as a young man and lived there for seven years before relocating to Niihau with his wife in 1939. Instantly at ease with the Japanese-American couple, Nishikaichi dropped the bombshell news about the attack on Pearl Harbor. The Haradas did not inform their neighbors.

That night, the hospitable Niihau residents learned about the Pearl Harbor attack on the radio. They decided to confine the pilot in the Haradas' home until help arrived.

An Example of Intercepted Japanese Espionage Plans

MESSAGE #067

Date: May 9, 1941

FROM: Los Angeles (Nakauchi)

TO: Tokyo (Gaimudaijin)

We have already established contacts with absolutely reliable Japanese in the San Pedro and San Diego area, who will keep a close watch on all shipments of airplanes and other war materials, and report the amounts and destinations of such shipments. The same steps have been taken with regard to traffic across the U.S.–Mexican border.

We shall maintain connection with our second-generations who are at present in the (U.S.) Army, to keep us informed of various developments in the Army. We also have connections with our second generations working in airplane plants for intelligence purposes.

David D. Lowman,
MAGIC: The Untold Story of U.S. Intelligence and the Evacuation of Japanese Residents from the West Coast During WW II, *2000.*

Exploiting their common ethnic ties and urging loyalty to the emperor [of Japan], Nishikaichi won over the Haradas. They enlisted the other resident of Japanese descent—the skittish Shintani—in a conspiracy to retrieve Nishikaichi's papers from Kaleohano. On the afternoon of December 12, a reluctant Shintani visited Kaleohano and asked for the enemy pilot's papers. He offered his neighbor a wad of cash. Kaleohano refused. Shintani desperately told him to burn the papers. It was a matter of life and death, Shintani pleaded with Kaleohano. Kaleohano again refused.

165

An hour later, Nishikaichi and the Haradas launched a campaign of terror against the islanders. They overtook the guard on duty and locked him in a warehouse. Mrs. Harada cranked up a phonograph to drown out the commotion. Yoshio Harada and Nishikaichi retrieved a shotgun from the warehouse and headed to Kaleohano's home. Kaleohano, who was in the outhouse, saw them coming and hid while Nishikaichi and his collaborators unsuccessfully searched for the pilot's papers. They recovered Nishikaichi's pistol and headed toward his grounded plane. Harada watched as the enemy pilot tried in vain to call for help on his radio.

A Night of Terror and Reprisal

Meanwhile, Kaleohano fled from the outhouse and ran to the main village to warn his neighbors of Nishikaichi's escape. He returned to his house to retrieve the papers, hid them in a relative's home, and set out with a strong team of islanders in a lifeboat toward Kauai to get help. That night, Harada and Nishikaichi set both the plane and Kaleohano's home on fire. They fired off their guns in a lunatic rage and threatened to kill every man, woman, and child in the village. After gathering for a prayer meeting, many residents escaped to a mountaintop with kerosene lamps and reflectors in an attempt to signal Kauai.

On the morning of December 13, Harada and Nishikaichi captured islander Ben Kanahele and his wife. Kanahele was ordered to find Kaleohano. In their own "Let's Roll" [Todd Beamer's last words on the doomed United Airlines Flight 93 of September 11] moment of heroism, the gutsy Kanaheles refused to cooperate. When Nishikaichi threatened to shoot Kanahele's wife, fifty-one-year-old Ben lunged for the enemy's shotgun. The young Japanese fighter pilot pulled his pistol from his boot and shot Kanahele three times in the chest, hip, and groin. Mrs. Kanahele pounced at Nishikaichi; her once-peaceful neighbor Harada tore her away.

Angered, the wounded Kanahele summoned the strength to pick up Nishikaichi and hurl him against a stone wall, knocking him unconscious. Quick-thinking Mrs. Kanahele grabbed a rock and pummeled the pilot's head. For good measure, Ben Kanahele took out a hunting knife and slit Nishikaichi's throat. A desperate Harada turned the shotgun on himself and committed suicide.

The Kanaheles' harrowing battle against a Japanese invader and his surprising collaborator was over.

The Case for Internment

The significance of the Haradas' stunning act of disloyalty and Shintani's meek complicity in collaboration with Nishikaichi was not lost on the Roosevelt administration. The facts of the case "indicate a strong possibility that other Japanese residents of the Territory of Hawaii [not yet a state], and Americans of Japanese descent . . . may give valuable aid to Japanese invaders in cases where the tide of battle is in favor of Japan and where it appears to residents that control of the district may shift from the United States to Japan," wrote Lieutenant C. B. Baldwin after a naval intelligence investigation.

The Haradas were neither radical nationalists nor professional spies. They were ordinary Japanese-Americans who betrayed America by putting their ethnic roots first. How many other Japanese-Americans—especially on the vulnerable West Coast—might be swayed by enemy appeals such as Nishikaichi's? How many more might be torn between allegiance for their country of birth and kinship with [Japanese] Imperial invaders? These were the daunting questions that faced the nation's top military and political leaders as enemy forces loomed on our shores.

"Racism and hysteria are irrational lenses through which people see their world, including its military threats."

Profiling Japanese Americans During World War II Was Unjustified

Eric Muller

In the following viewpoint, Eric Muller refutes the core arguments of Michelle Malkin's In Defense of Internment: The Case for "Racial Profiling" in World War II and the War on Terror. *He argues that Malkin relies on transcripts of intercepted telegrams to gauge the threat posed by Japanese espionage. According to Muller, this evidence does not reliably demonstrate that there were Japanese Americans working against U.S. interests during World War II, cannot justify the internment program, and fails to account for the extent of that program. Eric Muller is a professor at the University of North Carolina Law School and the author of several books on the Japanese-American experience during World War II.*

Eric Muller, "Indefensible Internment: There Was No Good Reason for the Mass Internment of Japanese Americans During WWII," *Reason*, vol. 36, no. 7, December 2004, http://www.reason.com. Reproduced by permission of *Reason* magazine and Reason.com.

As you read, consider the following questions:

1. Why does the author object to the internment of Japanese Americans based on the contents of the MAGIC telegrams?

2. Based on the evidence provided here, how would you characterize Lieutenant General John DeWitt's feelings toward Japanese Americans?

3. Why does the author argue that German Americans posed a greater threat of sabotage than Japanese Americans?

Since 9/11 [i.e., the September 11, 2001, terrorist attacks on the United States], some civil libertarians have denounced every antiterrorism policy that singles out Arab men as a repetition of the terrible mistake the government made after Pearl Harbor, when it evicted tens of thousands of American citizens of Japanese ancestry from their West Coast homes and banished them to barren camps in the interior. Supporters of profiling have a reasonable response to this comparison with what we've come to call the Japanese-American internment: There is a big difference between asking Arab male airline passengers some extra security questions and forcing American citizens behind barbed wire in the high desert for three years.

Malkin's Argument Is Not Historical

As obvious as that answer might seem, it is not the answer that conservative columnist Michelle Malkin gives in her book *In Defense of Internment: The Case for 'Racial Profiling' in World War II and the War on Terror*. She argues instead that the desert imprisonment of virtually all of the West Coast's Japanese-American men, women, and children for three years was the right thing to do: It was a sound military judgment that [President] Franklin Delano Roosevelt and his top war advisers made on the basis of solid intelligence that Japan had

Life on a Japanese-American Internment Camp

The internment camps were surrounded by barbed wire and guard towers. Armed guards patrolled the perimeter and were instructed to shoot anyone attempting to leave. The barracks consisted of tar paper over two-by-sixes and no insulation. Many families were assigned to one barracks and lived together with no privacy. Meals were taken communally in mess halls and required a long wait in line. A demonstration in [the] Manzanar [Camp] over the theft of food by personnel led to violence in which two died and many were injured. . . .

Throughout the course of World War II, not a single incident of espionage or treason was found to be committed by Japanese Americans.

Civil Liberties Public Education Fund, "Historical Overview of the Japanese American Internment." www.momomedia.com

organized untold numbers of Japanese resident aliens (the "Issei") and their American-citizen children (the "Nisei") into a vast network of spies and subversives.

Over the last several decades, historians have shown that the chief causes of the Japanese-American internment were ingrained anti-Asian racism, nativist and economic pressures from groups in California that had long wanted the Japanese gone, and the panic of wartime hysteria. As the Presidential Commission on the Wartime Relocation and Internment of Civilians said in its 1981 report to Congress, "The broad historical causes which shaped [the decisions to relocate and detain Japanese Americans] were race prejudice, war hysteria, and a failure of political leadership." Malkin contends that this history is a big lie—a "politically correct myth" that "has become enshrined as incontrovertible wisdom in the gullible press, postmodern academia, the cash-hungry grievance industry, and liberal Hollywood."

That passage alone should tell the reader this book is not a trustworthy work of history but a polemic [a strongly worded attack on an established belief]—*The O'Reilly Factor* masquerading as the History Channel. At the heart of Malkin's account are breathless allegations of widespread Japanese-American treason grounded primarily in the "MAGIC decrypts"—Japanese diplomatic cables that American military intelligence intercepted and decoded. These cables—to which President Roosevelt, Secretary of War Henry Stimson, and his assistant John J. McCloy had access—revealed what Malkin describes as a "meticulously orchestrated espionage effort to undermine our national security [that] utilized both Issei and Nisei, in Hawaii and on the West Coast, before and after the Pearl Harbor attack." It was primarily this intelligence, says Malkin, rather than racism or wartime hysteria, that led this trio of men to approve and implement the eviction, exclusion, and detention of all people of Japanese ancestry along the West Coast.

Malkin's Scant Evidence Cannot Support the Claims

Malkin's evidence simply does not support the enormous weight of the argument that she builds on it. First, many of the men who proposed and implemented the internment did not have access to the ultra-secret MAGIC cables. [Lieutenant General] John DeWitt, the chief architect of the eviction of Japanese Americans, did not see them. Neither did the governors of the Mountain West states, who in April 1942 rejected the federal government's request to allow Japanese Americans freedom of movement and instead insisted that any Japanese Americans in their states be kept behind barbed wire and under military guard. Plainly, the MAGIC intelligence could not have influenced them.

More important, we know nothing at all about how the few men who did have access to the tens of thousands of decrypted cables actually used them or understood them.

Nothing in the historical record shows that Roosevelt, Stimson, or McCloy attached any particular significance to any specific MAGIC decrypt, let alone to the vanishingly tiny fraction that mentioned a desire to enlist Nisei spies.

What this means is that the evidence Malkin deploys to "debunk the great myth of the 'Japanese American internment' as 'racist' and 'unjustified'" is—at best—mere speculation. This speculation might be worth a moment's reflection if Malkin also addressed the voluminous historical research that has shown the impact of racism, nativism, political pressure, economic jealousies, and war panic on the government's policies toward Japanese Americans.

The Existence of a Real Domestic Japanese Threat Is Questionable

Greg Robinson, for example, a historian at the University of Quebec at Montreal, carefully traces the development of Roosevelt's view of Japanese Americans as immutably foreign and dangerous in his 2001 book *By Order of the President: FDR and the Internment of Japanese Americans*. And at least half a dozen works by Roger Daniels, a historian at the University of Cincinnati, document the intense lobbying for evacuation by California nativist groups and white agricultural interests as well as the extraordinary viciousness of America's leading newspaper columnists in demanding that Japanese Americans (in the words of one of them) be "herded up, packed off, and given the inside room in the Badlands."

But Malkin does not so much as mention any of that evidence, except to say that a reader can find it elsewhere in "pedantic tomes" and "educational propaganda." She dismisses what she cannot rebut.

These objections to Malkin's handling of the evidence are the concerns of scholars and historians, and some may think them unfair measures for the work of a political columnist. "I am neither a historian nor a lawyer," Malkin reminds her reader in the book's prefatory note. But even political columnists are bound by ordinary rules of inference and logic, and it is on this score that her book fails even more spectacularly.

Even Risk of Espionage Could Not Justify the Internment

Let us posit, for the sake of argument, that FDR [President Franklin D. Roosevelt] relied on concrete evidence of Japanese-American spying when, in mid-February of 1942, he signed the executive order that authorized the military to exclude people from sensitive military areas. At most, that would mean that the government had a basis for doing *something* to detect and prevent Japanese-American spying. It would not mean that the government had a basis for doing *what it actually did*, which was to evict more than 110,000 people of Japanese ancestry (including tens of thousands of U.S. citizens) from their homes without charges or hearings, exclude them from the entire coastal region, and detain them in desolate camps for years after any threat of a Japanese assault on the U.S. mainland had evaporated.

The financial costs to Japanese Americans were enormous; estimates run well above $150 million (in 1940s dollars) for property loss alone, and that figure does not include loss of income or opportunity. Neither, of course, does it reflect the incalculable emotional losses Japanese Americans suffered through stigmatization and incarceration. Almost all of the financial losses went uncompensated; a government program for paying claims for documented property loss ultimately paid out an average of 25 cents on every claimed dollar. Token redress payments of $20,000 to surviving internees in the late 1980s were a pittance given the actual losses. Surely a handful

of ambiguous diplomatic messages cannot support the inflic-
tion of this amount of suffering.

Malkin might have written a book called *In Defense of
Limited Measures to Protect Against Japanese-American Subver-
sion*. But she instead wrote *In Defense of Internment*. This is
not a technical distinction. What supported the *confinement* of
Japanese Americans through 1942, 1943, 1944, and a good
part of 1945? It was certainly not the MAGIC cables, or any
other intelligence source.

What supported it was instead the sort of view that [Lieu-
tenant General] DeWitt expressed in 1942, when he said that
"the Japanese race is an enemy race, and while many second
and third generation Japanese born on United States soil, pos-
sessed of United States citizenship, have become 'Americanized,'
the racial strains are undiluted." What supported it was the
sort of opinion voiced by California Attorney General (later
U.S. Supreme Court Chief Justice) Earl Warren when he argued that the *absence* of subversive activity by Japanese Americans proved that such activity was just around the corner.
What supported it, in other words, was racism and wartime
hysteria.

Japanese Americans Imprisoned, German Americans Ignored

And what supported the government's decision to force all
American citizens of Japanese ancestry into camps for years
while taking no programmatic action of any sort against
American citizens of German or Italian ancestry? It is important to remember that while Lou Shimizu and Joe Takahashi
sat in desert camps, Lou Gehrig and Joe DiMaggio played
baseball. This was a breathtaking discrimination among U.S.
citizens who shared every cause for suspicion except for their
race.

Malkin justifies this discrimination as a military measure
in a single paragraph, contending that our European enemies

posed a lesser threat to the U.S. mainland than the Japanese and had fewer spies, and that American citizens of German and Italian parentage would have been too logistically difficult to exclude because of their large numbers. These justifications defy reason.

Germany was a more dangerous presence along the East Coast of the U.S. mainland for a far longer time than was Japan along the West Coast, and it twice landed saboteurs on Eastern shores. Germany had a network of spies whose existence did not need to be pieced together from vague references in decrypted diplomatic messages. And as for Malkin's point that there were so many potential German-American and Italian-American saboteurs on the East Coast that it made sense to do nothing to them—well, that argument refutes itself.

Defending Internment Camps

Lurking behind Malkin's book is a more basic error about the way human beings make decisions. Malkin writes about a world in which the president and his military advisers acted primarily because of *either* clear military threats *or* racism and hysteria. But of course that is not how racism and hysteria work. Racism and hysteria are irrational lenses through which people see their world, including its military threats. Malkin writes as though it were possible to wring prejudice and panic from the minds of the military men who planned and executed the Japanese-American internment. To say that racist and hysterical planners may have believed it was necessary to evict and detain tens of thousands of innocent Americans is one thing. To say, as Malkin does, that these planners truly were motivated by cool assessment of solid intelligence is quite another.

In the final analysis, *In Defense of Internment* is a book that did not need writing. When she finally gets around to proposing antiterrorism policy in the last chapter of her book,

175

Malkin advocates such measures as allowing law enforcement and airport security to take account of ethnicity, and barring Muslims from serving in combat roles in the Middle East. To support these measures, she had no need to take up the cause of defending the lengthy and miserable detention of tens of thousands of innocent American citizens of Japanese ancestry.

Why, then, did she choose to take up that cause, and why now? Could it be that she actually supports the idea of detaining American Arabs and Muslims? "Make no mistake," she says in her book, "I am not advocating rounding up all Arabs or Muslims and tossing them into camps."

Forgive me the mistake.

"The public displays a common sense desire to improve health through many viable pathways and has moved past politically correct clichés."

Racial Profiling Is Medically Useful

Sally Satel

In the following viewpoint, Sally Satel gives several examples of studies that demonstrate certain broad, biological differences among people of different races. She argues that rather than ignore this information, doctors should incorporate it into their practice to provide their patients with the best possible care. Sally Satel is a psychiatrist and the author of several books, in-cluding The Health Disparities Myth: Diagnosing the Treat-ment Gap *and* PC, M.D.: How Political Correctness Is Cor-rupting Medicine.

As you read, consider the following questions:

1. What is BiDil and why is it significant?
2. According to the author, what percentages of blacks and whites were found to have refused surgery in a 2003 lung cancer study?

Sally Satel, "Smoking Out Cliches About Race," *Medical Progress Today*, February 2, 2006. Reproduced by permission of the publisher and the author.

3. What two behaviors does the author believe may contribute to African American smokers' heightened risk of developing lung cancer?

Cigarette smoke may not be an equal opportunity carcinogen. According to a [2006 report in the] *New England Journal of Medicine*, the same amount of cigarette smoke was associated with higher rates of lung cancer in African-Americans and Native Hawaiians than other groups. Despite comparable low-to-moderate exposure, whites were about half as likely to develop lung cancer and Latinos and Asians were about half as likely as whites to develop it.

The study certainly has health implications. "If you're an African-American and you think that by smoking 10 cigarettes a day that you're not going to be at increased risk of developing lung cancer, this study shows that you are," Dr. Joseph Cicenia, a pulmonologist at St. Vincent's Hospital Manhattan told the *New York Daily News*.

The Debate About Race and Biology

But the study also has political implications. It rekindles a story line that BiDil brought into the spotlight recently. Approved by the FDA [Food and Drug Administration] last June for the treatment of heart failure, BiDil—a combination drug containing a diuretic (hydralazine) and a nitric oxide enhancer (isosorbide dinitrate)—made headlines because it is the first drug ever to have been approved for use in a racial group, African Americans.

BiDil was demonstrated to be especially effective in black patients, most likely because of aspects of blood pressure physiology that vary by race. For reasons not well understood, individuals of African heritage are, on average, less likely to produce or release the molecule nitric oxide from the cells that line blood vessels, thus contributing to hypertension. Isosorbide seems to work by releasing nitric oxide at the blood vessel wall.

Race, Genetics, and Disease

Understanding the relation between race and genetic variation has important practical implications. Several of the polymorphisms [tiny genetic variations] that differ in frequency from group to group have specific effects on health. The mutations responsible for sickle cell disease and some cases of cystic fibrosis, for instance, result from genetic changes that appear to have risen in frequency because they were protective against diseases prevalent in Africa and Europe, respectively. . . .

Genetic variation also plays a role in individual susceptibility to . . . AIDS [acquired immune deficiency syndrome]. Some people have a small deletion in both their copies of a gene that encodes a particular cell-surface receptor called chemokine receptor 5 (CCR5). As a result, these individuals fail to produce CCR5 receptors on the surface of their cells. Most strains of HIV-1, the virus that causes AIDS, bind to the CCR5 receptor to gain entry to cells, so people who lack CCR5 receptors are resistant to HIV-1 infection. This polymorphism in the CCR5 receptor gene is found almost exclusively in groups from northeastern Europe.

Several polymorphisms in CCR5 do not prevent infection but instead influence the rate at which HIV-1 infection leads to AIDS and death. . . . One polymorphism, for example is associated with delayed disease progression in European-Americans but accelerated disease in African-Americans. Researchers can only study such population-specific effects—and use that knowledge to direct therapy—if they can sort people into groups.

Michael Bamshad and Steve Olson,
Scientific American, *December 2003.*

Naturally, news of BiDil's clinical promise inflamed the debate about the extent to which race has biological aspects. And, sure enough, the new lung cancer study provoked similar reactions.

"This feeds into the 19th-century notion that these categories really separate people in terms of their physical and biological characteristics," said Troy Duster of New York University. (Only the most scientifically illiterate today believe this straw man of race. As early as the 1770's, Johann Friedrich Blumenbach, considered the father of physical anthropology, remarked that "innumerable varieties of mankind run into each other by insensible degrees.")

Bioethicist Jeffrey Kahn of the University of Minnesota told the *Washington Post* that he worried the findings could be used to further discriminate: "The danger would be to sort of view lung cancer as a minority disease, and so something we don't have to worry as much about."

Health Disparities and Doctor Bias

Kahn can calm down. The issue of "health disparities" is thriving. The Department of Health and Human Services has made it a priority area and health organizations like Robert Wood Johnson, Kaiser and Commonwealth Foundations have placed it high on their agendas. Unfortunately, though, part of the campaign to understand and combat differences in health status by race often includes an effort to eradicate physician bias. The idea of doctor bias acquired considerable and unmerited weight in both academic literature and the popular press. It enjoyed a great boost in visibility from a 2002 report from the Institute of Medicine, part of the National Academy of Sciences, called *Unequal Treatment: Confronting Racial and Ethnic Disparities in Health Care*, widely hailed as the authoritative study on health disparities. It concluded that the dynamics of the doctor-patient relationship—"bias," "prejudice," and "discrimination"—were a significant cause of the treatment differential and, by extension, of the poorer health of minorities.

Satisfying as this explanation may be for some people, it is wrong. Racially biased doctors are not a cause of poor minority health—a proposition almost impossible to prove in any case. It is the socioeconomic factors associated with race that generate the strongest momentum in driving the differences between races in both care and outcomes. Indeed, for answers to the race-related differences in health care, it turns out that the doctor's office is not the most rewarding place to look. White and black patients, on average, do not even visit the same population of physicians—making the idea of preferential treatment by individual doctors a far less compelling explanation for disparities in health.

Doctors whom black patients tend to see may not be in a position to provide optimal care. Furthermore, because health care varies a great deal depending on where people live, and because blacks are overrepresented in regions of the United States served by poorer health care facilities, disparities are destined to be, at least in part, a function of residence. Nonetheless, many medical schools, health philanthropies, policymakers, and politicians are proceeding as if physician "bias" were an established fact.

Cultural Differences Create Health Disparities

Lung cancer was the subject of "bias" speculation when Peter Bach and colleagues at Memorial Sloan Kettering Cancer Center published a 1999 study in which they examined records of over 10,000 Medicare [federally sponsored health care for those over-65] patients who received diagnoses of operable lung cancer. Seventy-seven percent of white patients underwent surgery compared with 64% of black patients. Five years later, one-third of the white patients, but only one-quarter of the black patients, were still alive.

Those numbers understandably aroused concern, but many unanswered questions remained. One question was whether black patients refuse surgery more often than whites? The answer is yes. In 2003 researchers at the Philadelphia Veterans Affairs Medical Center presented their survey of over six hundred patients with pulmonary disease from three veterans hospital sites across the country. They found that more blacks than whites (61 percent versus 29 percent) maintained the folk belief that the spread of lung cancer was accelerated when the tumor was exposed to air during surgery and would oppose surgery because of this (19 percent versus 5 percent). A study of patients with operable lung cancer conducted at Detroit's Henry Ford Health System found refusal of surgery by black patients over three times more common than by whites. (Both whites and blacks were offered the surgery at similar rates.)

These studies are just a sample showing the concern of researchers with the social determinants of racial health differentials. In fact, big differences in health status are traceable to access to care and health literacy which is, in turn, a reflection of socioeconomic status, not race per se. [A 2006] *New York Times* front page series on diabetes in the inner city captured it all—biological predispositions among blacks and Hispanics to type II diabetes coupled with the chaotic lives, the priorities of life that crowd out health concerns for poor people, the perverse Medicaid [federally funded health care for the poor] reimbursement schemes to providers wherein they get short-changed on vital preventive care, (e.g., podiatric care; nutritional guidance).

Study Raises Important Questions of Biology and Race

[A February 2005] *New England Journal [of Medicine]* article on lung cancer rates is judicious. The authors control for factors that might vary by group and influence the likelihood of developing cancer (e.g., occupation, diet, level of education) and they did find some differences but not of sufficient magnitude to account for the cancer disparities. Notably, nonsmokers, irrespective of ethnic or racial group, had the same incidence of lung cancer. The theory that blacks are "constitutionally more susceptible" to the carcinogens in tobacco smoke is put forth alongside the possibility that blacks, as a group, may have a unique smoking style. Studies have shown they tend to inhale cigarette smoke more frequently and more deeply; perhaps, as well, the use of mentholated cigarettes (more popular among black smokers) is relevant.

Researchers, physicians and readers of newspaper health stories appreciate the complexity of race. That is, at minimum, they grasp that social aspects and biological aspects are intertwined. One can't help but think that it is the professional handwringers, like sociologist Duster and bioethicist Kahn, who keep worrying the thorn of racial discrimination. The public displays a common sense desire to improve health through many viable pathways and has moved past politically correct clichés.

"*Diseases commonly considered bounded by race, such as sickle cell anemia, are not.*"

Racial Profiling Is Medically Useless

Robert Lee Hotz

In the following viewpoint, Robert Lee Hotz warns against allowing our growing understanding of the human genome to seduce us into once again relying on sloppy, deterministic notions of race. Hotz points out that although such observable phenomena as skin color are clearly the result of a person's genetic make-up, researchers must work to translate the nuances of genetic difference into medically useful methods without feeding into race-based assumptions. Pulitzer Prize-winning science journalist Robert Lee Hotz has been writing about the intersection of science, politics, and culture since the mid-1970s.

As you read, consider the following questions:

1. On average, how much genetic overlap does the author say is present between any two human beings?

Robert Lee Hotz, "Scientists Using Maps of Genes for Therapies Are Wary of Profiling," *The Wall Street Journal*, October 26, 2007. Reprinted with permission of *The Wall Street Journal*.

2. What did the editors of the *New England Journal of Medicine* determine about race in 2002?

3. According to researchers cited by Hotz, what portion of the genes of an average white Brazilian are inherited from Africans?

There is little of black and white in the human genome. We are so new as a species—about 150,000 years—that there is less genetic difference between any two of us than between any two members of almost any other mammalian species. Whatever our ethnic identity, we share 99% of our DNA with each other.

Yet, in that other one percent, researchers are finding so many individual differences they promise to transform the practice of medicine, enabling treatments targeted to our own unique DNA code. Viewed through the prism of our genes, we each have a spectrum of variation in which a single molecular misstep can alter the risk of disease or the effectiveness of therapy.

The Inaccuracy of Race Labels Hinders Medicine

[In October 2007] the International HapMap Consortium, a group of research institutes and universities in six countries, reported discovery of 2.1 million places along the human genome where our genetic code—fugues of [DNA components] AGCT—varies by just a single letter from person to person, tripling the known variations in just two years.

As researchers delve deeper into the biochemistry of human variation, however, we lack the vocabulary to talk about these distinctions clearly. Scientists and doctors struggle for ways to translate the nuances of genetic identity into racially defined medical treatments without reviving misconceptions about the significance, for example, of skin color.

The problem arises because it may be decades before anyone can afford their own genetic medical profile. Meanwhile,

Ancestry Is Not Race; Ancestry Is Medically Useful

Attributing racial labels to DNA samples is well on its way to acceptance in forensics and law enforcement. Application in medicine is likely forthcoming, but has arguably greater potential to cause harm, as misuse of genetic information about race in medical applications could severely undermine the public's confidence in the application of genetics to health. Referring to "geographic ancestry" instead of race is an emerging alternative that is both more accurate and less contentious. One way to operationalize this approach is for the National Institutes of Health to change its current requirement to use Office of Management and Budget categories and instead mandate stratification of individuals by self-assessed descriptors of ancestry such as the geographic origin of an individual's parents (e.g., Central Africa, Southeast Asia, Central America), followed by their ethnic identity, and finally the community in which a person resides. This strategy might not differ much from existing practices—particularly for individuals who know little about their origins—but it underscores the need to take account of biogeographic ancestry, it de-emphasizes the use of racial categories, and it may be a better interim solution to making ancestry inferences in the absence of explicit genetic data. In the end, however, every human being is genetically unique and so must be treated as an individual, not an example of a group defined by geography or race.

Mike Bamshad,
Journal of the American Medical Association,
August 24 2005.

doctors expect to rely on racial profiling as a diagnostic tool to identify those at genetic risk of chronic diseases or adverse reactions to prescription drugs.

Researchers at Brown University and the University of London, and the editors of the journal *PLoS Medicine*, [in September 2007] warned about inaccurate racial labels in clinical research. In the absence of meaningful population categories, researchers may single out an inherited racial linkage where none exists, or overlook the medical effects of our environment: what we eat, where we live and how we treat each other. "This is a debate over how medicine will be practiced in the 21st century," said gender biologist Anne Fausto-Sterling at Brown University.

Race Categories Do Not Work Well

It's not the first time that medical authorities have raised a red flag about racial labels. In 1995, the American College of Physicians urged its 85,000 members to drop racial labels in patient case studies because "race has little or no utility in careful medical thinking." In 2002, the editors of the *New England Journal of Medicine* concluded that "'race' is biologically meaningless." And in 2004, the editors of *Nature Genetics* warned that "it's bad medicine and it's bad science."

No one denies the social reality of race, as reinforced by history, or the role of heredity. At its most extreme, however, the concept of race encompasses the idea that test scores, athletic ability, or character is rooted in the genetic chemistry of people who can be grouped by skin color. That's simply wrong, research shows. Indeed, such outmoded beliefs led to the resignation [October 2007] of Nobel laureate James Watson [co-discoverer of the structure of DNA] from the Cold Spring Harbor Laboratory in New York, for disparaging comments he made about Africans.

Diseases commonly considered bounded by race, such as sickle cell anemia, are not. Some of the highest rates of sickle cell occur among India's Pardhan and Oktar peoples, not Africans. It's also common in Sicily and Greece. Yet, clinical studies routinely analyze the data of personal variation in broad brush strokes, without regard for the vast range of genetic variation that ancestry may encompass.

Researchers studying physical appearance and genetic ancestry in Brazil, for example, discovered that people with white skin owed almost a third of their genes, on average, to African ancestry, while those with dark skin could trace almost half of their genes to Europe, they reported in the *Proceedings of the National Academy of Sciences.* "It's clear that the categories we use don't work very well," said Stanford University biomedical ethicist Mildred Cho.

Researchers Cling to Race

Government reporting requirements in the U.S. heighten the difficulty. Since 2001, clinical researchers must use groupings identified by the U.S. Census that don't recognize the underlying complexities of individual variation, migration and family ancestry. In addition, medical reports in the PubMed, Medline and the U.S. National Library of Medicine databases were cataloged until 2003 by discredited 19th-century racial terms.

Today, there are no rigorous, standardized scientific categories. A recent study of 120 genetics and heredity journals found that only two had guidelines for race and ethnic categories, though half of them had published articles that used such labels to analyze findings.

Eventually, genomics may eliminate any medical need for the infectious shorthand of race. "We need to find the underlying causes of disease," said David Goldstein, at Duke University's Center for Population Genomics & Pharmacogenetics. "Once we do, nobody will care about race and ethnicity anymore."

Periodical Bibliography

The following articles have been selected to supplement the diverse views presented in this chapter.

John Caher	"Racial Profiling Case Begins in N.Y.," *The Legal Intelligencer*, October 27, 2005.
Adriane Fugh-Berman	"Why Race-Based Medicine Is a Bad Idea," *Women's Health Activist*, September-October 2005.
Malcolm Gladwell	"Troublemakers: What Pit Bulls Can Teach Us About Profiling," *The New Yorker*, February 6, 2006.
John Leo	"The Internment Taboo," *US News & World Report*, September 19, 2004.
Andy Lindstrom	"Roosevelt's Wrong Enemies: In a Hasty Move Made in the Name of National Security, FDR Needlessly Swept Some 4,000 Civilians from Their Homes in Latin America," *Florida Trend*, August 2004.
Eric Muller	"A Troubling Partial Rehabilitation of *Korematsu v. United States*," *Is That Legal?*, January 14, 2008. http://www.isthatlegal.org/archives/2008/01/a_troubling_par.html.
William Raspberry	"Why Profiling Won't Work," *Washington Post*, August 22, 2005.
Richard G. Schott	"The Role of Race in Law Enforcement: Racial Profiling or Legitimate Use?" *Law Enforcement Bulletin*, November 2001.
Paul Sperry	"When the Profile Fits the Crime," *New York Times*, July 28, 2005.
Cathy Young	"Defending Repression: Why Are Conservatives Trying to Rehabilitate McCarthyism and the Japanese Internment?" *Reason*, November 2004.

CHAPTER 4

What Are the Consequences of Racial Profiling?

Chapter Preface

In September 2002, Maher Arar, a Canadian telecommunications engineer, was stopped and questioned during a layover at John F. Kennedy (JFK) airport in New York. Although born in Syria, Arar had moved to Canada as a teenager and been a Canadian citizen for more than a decade. On that day he was flying from Zurich, Switzerland, to his home in Canada. He never got on his connecting flight.

Arar spent the next two weeks in U.S. custody. He was repeatedly questioned for hours at a time with no access to legal counsel, then finally deported. Due to false information furnished by Canadian authorities, Arar was deported not to his home country of Canada but to his birth country of Syria. There he was held in solitary confinement for almost a year, in a dark three-by-six-foot cell, and regularly tortured.

As it turned out, there was no real reason to suspect Arar of anything. Canadian authorities had noted that Arar very occasionally associated with a "person of interest" in one of their terror investigations, Abdullah Almalki. Almalki was the brother of one of Arar's former coworkers; his family was also Syrian and had immigrated to Canada at about the same time as Arar's. Abdullah Almalki has never been accused of any wrongdoing. In 2006, a Canadian commission completely exonerated Arar. Justice Dennis O'Connor, head of that commission, concluded that he was "able to say categorically that there is no evidence to indicate that Mr. Arar has committed any offense or that his activities constitute a threat to the security of Canada."

Nonetheless, when Arar passed through immigration at JFK airport one year after the terrorist attacks of September 11, agents saw an Arab Muslim who had been associated with a "person of interest" in a Canadian investigation, both of whom were born in a country designated by the U.S. State

Department as a "state sponsor of terror." There was no evidence against Arar, apart from some cursory biographical details on him and his occasional lunch companion. Arar lost a year of his life to beatings and fear; the U.S. and Canadian governments wasted countless dollars and hours; both governments were embarrassed in the international media; and the Canadian government ultimately had to pay Arar $12.5 million in compensation for what he had endured. A little guesswork based on the terrorist profile had enormous consequences for everyone involved.

It is difficult to assess the full cost of racial profiling, taking into account monetary costs, time wasted, suffering endured, the loss of trust in law enforcement, and the degradation of the United States' standing in the international community. The authors of the following viewpoints examine the breadth of consequences that racial profiling carries.

"*Many residents have come to accept the harassment from Border Patrol as a regular feature of border life.*"

Profiling Endangers Law-Abiding Citizens

Anmol Chaddha

In the following viewpoint, Anmol Chaddha argues that post-9/11 interest in securing the southern border of the United States from terrorist infiltration has in actuality mainly focused on preventing Hispanic workers from illegally entering the country. He argues that the increasingly militarized presence along the border has fostered suspicion of all Latinos—even those who are natural-born U.S. citizens—and encourages vigilantism. Anmol Chaddha is a graduate student in sociology and social policy at Harvard University.

As you read, consider the following questions:

1. According to the author, what percentage of the residents of Douglas, Arizona, are Latino?

Anmol Chaddha, "Borderland Security: Vigilantes Are Far from the Fringe in Arizona—Instead Organizers Say, Ranchers and Border Agents Mirror a Violent Border Society Where Racial Profiling Abounds and Prosecution of Abuse Is Rare," *ColorLines Magazine*, vol. 6, no. 4, Winter 2003, pp. 30–32. © 2003 *ColorLines Magazine*. Reproduced by permission.

2. According to the county attorney, how many migrants pass through Cochise County, Arizona, each month? What does he compare this number to?

3. According to Isabel Garcia, why doesn't the U.S. government crack down on vigilantism at the border?

Thirteen-year-old Rosita Gonzales heard strange noises while she and her brothers were playing in a tent they had set up in the backyard. She grabbed her backpack and ran toward the house. Behind her home in Pirtleville, AZ, a tiny desert town on the U.S.-Mexico border, the Border Patrol agents [now an agency of the Department of Homeland Security] who were prowling in the brush assumed the girl to be a fleeing undocumented migrant and opened fire, shattering her kneecap. Although she survived the shooting, the incident became one of many incidents that have created and maintained an atmosphere of violence and harassment throughout towns near the southern Arizona border.

Life for Latino Americans on the Border

This past year, community organizers with the Border Action Network (BAN) went door to door in border towns like Douglas, AZ, to assess how the increasingly active presence of Border Patrol agents has affected the lives of the city's 15,000 residents—an estimated 93 percent of whom are Latino. They heard stories of relentless harassment by local law enforcement and Border Patrol agents who flagrantly racially profile local residents, previously quiet neighborhoods made unsafe by Border Patrol vehicles carelessly speeding through the streets, and physical abuse and intimidation that painted a picture of what Jennifer Allen, executive director of BAN, describes as "low-intensity warfare." And in this war on migrants, the residents of towns like Douglas have been unwillingly placed on the front lines.

Local residents also expressed fear of the vigilante groups [self-appointed "law enforcement" groups who have no legal authority] that have emerged in tandem with the rapid expansion of Border Patrol activity in this region. These groups of white ranchers and other sympathetic nativists believe that the federal government is coming up short in its efforts to crack down on undocumented migrants, and they are determined to take on the responsibility of patrolling the borders themselves. Promoting themselves as patriots protecting American jobs and defending national security, particularly in a post-9/11 context, the camouflage-clad vigilantes routinely stop groups of migrants at gunpoint, demand to know their immigration status, order them to the ground, and detain them until Border Patrol agents arrive.

Despite concerns about human rights violations by groups acting as extralegal law enforcement outfits, local authorities have failed to prosecute any of the ranchers. While mainstream media outlets and local public officials portray these groups as fringe elements, vigilantes and Border Patrol agents occupy essentially the same piece of a violent border society. "The vigilante groups emerge within a larger political climate that says it's OK to hunt people down at gunpoint," Allen explains. "The Border Patrol does the same thing regularly."

Background on Illegal Immigration in Douglas

Over the past decade, the Border Patrol has implemented its Southwest Border Strategy, which has entailed the construction of longer and taller walls and fences in an attempt to seal off the major points of entry and increasing the number of agents patrolling these areas. San Diego and El Paso were the first high-traffic areas targeted by the agency through [pre-9/11] Operation Gatekeeper and Operation Hold the Line. But rather than reducing the scale of migration across the Southern border, this strategy has had the effect of pushing hopeful migrants away from these cities and forcing them to cross in desert regions under life-threatening conditions of extreme heat and no access to water.

Along the border, smaller towns like Douglas, in Arizona's Cochise County, have witnessed a dramatic influx of migrants who are discouraged from entering near the larger cities. County Attorney Chris Roll says he began noticing the increase around 1998, and that by 2000, the number of migrants passing through the county every month matched the county's total population of 115,000. Roll explains that the agency's strategies "tend to simply move the problem around from one area to another." Instead of deterring migration altogether, the Border Patrol's strategy amounts to a cat and mouse game on the Southern Border that is being played with the lives of undocumented migrants and town residents.

With increased migration in Cochise County, the Border Patrol's response has been to beef up the presence of agents in towns like Douglas, which has again pushed the migrants to cross even more obscure and dangerous terrain, as evidenced by the ballooning migrant deaths along the Arizona border in recent years. In 2001, 78 migrants died along the border in Arizona, according to Border Patrol figures. The next year the number jumped to 134, and [in 2003], 139 migrants . . . died while attempting to cross the border.

[In 2003], the Border Patrol opened its new subsector in Douglas with a tall watch-tower that marks the landscape and greets drivers as they reach the town on Highway 80. According to the Border Patrol, about 1,600 agents are spread across all of the Tucson Sector, which includes Douglas. The owner of a local coffee shop in Douglas observes that a few years ago "there were only about 10 guards posted here. Now, there are hundreds." And in such a short time, they have made a profound mark on the consciousness of the local community. While Border Patrol SUVs seem to pass by every 10 minutes, one longtime resident added that "half of the regular cars you see are unmarked Border Patrol, too. It's basically become a police state."

Profiling at the Border

In a town where nearly all of the residents share the same skin color as the "illegals" that the agents are trained to hunt, the implications of this Border Patrol presence have been far-reaching. Douglas residents told BAN organizers about how, while driving through the town in which they were born, they are routinely pulled over and required to show their IDs. Mothers explained that they do not allow their children to play outside because Border Patrol vehicles recklessly careen through neighborhoods, and many community members described being stopped by Border Patrol agents while shopping at the local Wal-Mart that stands just five blocks from the border.

While organizers noted that many residents have come to accept the harassment from Border Patrol as a regular feature of border life, community members repeatedly mentioned their fear of the vigilante groups, which have been especially active in Cochise County. They believed that anyone with brown skin was a target and cited perpetrators such as Roger Barnett, a local rancher whose vigilante activity has been well documented by media, community groups, and the Mexican Consul stationed in Douglas.

On a Sunday afternoon in January 2003, for example, Barnett confronted a Mexican migrant who was walking alongside Highway 80. Rodrigo Acosta was overcome with thirst and had decided to turn himself in to the Border Patrol, according to Mexican Consulate reports. After being stopped by the rancher, Acosta was punched, kicked, and hit in the head with a battery lamp. When he tried to run away, he was chased and bitten by dogs before Barnett caught him. Since 1999, the Mexican Consul has documented 31 incidents involving Barnett in which he has detained 484 migrants; Barnett claims to have captured more than 5,000. . . .

The Psychological Impact

As many of the cases reported to AIUSA (Amnesty International USA) illustrate, there is a significant amount of empirical data suggesting a strong correlation between racial profiling and excessive use of force. However, even when excessive force is not involved, incidents of racial profiling often have a long-lasting impact on their victims. Individuals who reported such incidents to AIUSA during the last 12 months frequently cited:

- feelings of humiliation, depression, helplessness, anger, and fear

- diminished trust in law enforcement

- reluctance to turn to law enforcement for help

People who witnessed such incidents, especially those that involved excessive force, frequently said they had been affected in similar ways. One man, whose young daughter witnessed him being pepper sprayed by a police officer during a profiling incident, said that she now frequently cries when she sees a police officer.

"Threat and Humiliation: Racial Profiling,
Domestic Security, and Human Rights in the United States,"
Amnesty International USA, October 2004. www.amnestyusa.org

Vigilantes and Border Patrol Disregard Human Rights

Far from acting as fringe elements in the border society, vigilantism in Arizona is more accurately described as a logical outgrowth of the Border Patrol's Southwest Border Strategy. Heightening the militarization at urban areas along the border fails to address any of the underlying economic and geopolitical inequalities that define the reality of migration at the Southern Border. In areas of Cochise County, nativist ranchers are influenced by anti-immigrant federal policy and react violently to migrants passing over their property on the way to opportunities that might allow the migrants to sustain themselves and their families. As one Cochise County resident explained, "You are looking at people who were barely making it in ranching and rural industries when the federal border policy pushed them over the limit."

In terms of their tactics, the vigilante groups seem to be following the lead of Border Patrol agents who routinely stop individuals on the basis of skin color, round people up at gun point, and physically intimidate and abuse migrants. Despite the high publicity of vigilante activity and extensive documentation of the incidents by advocacy groups and the Mexican government, very few cases have ever been prosecuted against vigilante incidents across Arizona. "The government has refused to act because these guys are simply acting out what our federal immigration policy says," explains Isabel Garcia of Derechos Humanos, an immigrant advocacy group in Arizona.

Critics also point to the dehumanization of migrants that underpins federal border policy. The portrayal of migrants as involved in the drug trade contributes to the space immigrants occupy in the public imagination, as do the Border Patrol guidelines that warn local residents not to provide medical aid to stranded migrants because providing transportation to a hospital is considered "illegal and can result in prosecution."

"They cease to be human and their lives and families are confined to three letters—UDA [undocumented alien]," says BAN director Allen.

A spokesperson for the Border Patrol in Tucson explains that the agency recognizes "the right of the [vigilante] groups to exist." She goes on to offer a seemingly contradictory message by stating that the "Border Patrol discourages people from taking matters into their own hands," while they "encourage people to call us if they come across someone they suspect is undocumented." This ambivalence contributes to the notion that private citizens can and should function to uphold federal immigration policy.

Suspicion and Fear Are "Normal"

A large sign at the corner of a ranch along a stretch of Highway 80 just outside Douglas reads: "Terrorists Love Open Borders." While Arizona might seem like an unlikely site to measure post-9/11 fallout, it does occupy a space at the forefront with two immigration detention centers in the small town of Florence, another in Eloy, and an immigration detention center for children located in Phoenix. Nearly one out of 10 detained immigrants in the United States is held in these Arizona facilities.

Arizona is also home to active organizing from groups such as the Florence Immigrant and Refugee Rights Project, Humane Borders, Derechos Humanos, and the Border Action Network. Republican congressmen from this state are proposing shifts to immigration policy through a controversial guest-worker bill that does little to protect or improve the lives of migrants themselves and focuses instead on their role as producers in the U.S. economy.

As the federal government uses the cover of "homeland security" to round up, detain and deport immigrants across the country, private ranchers in Arizona use the justification of national security to round up and detain people themselves.

While President Bush has explicitly legitimated the use of racial profiling in the interest of national security, border towns provide a look into communities where the lives of local residents have been defined by racial profiling and harassment for years. Allen explains, "People in these border towns come to accept these practices as normal. That's just border life."

VIEWPOINT

"*Democratic and Republican members of Congress alike used arguments exaggerating . . . the extent to which the UAE [United Arab Emirates] has been connected to terrorism.*"

Racial Profiling Disrupts Commerce

NewStandard

In the following viewpoint, NewStandard recounts the controversial 2006 case of Dubai Ports World, which was poised to begin operating six U.S. ports when it assumed control of a British company. Dubai Ports World is owned by the Middle Eastern country United Arab Emirates, causing both Republicans and Democrats in Congress to raise homeland security concerns. NewStandard argues that Congress's concerns about terrorism constituted ethnic profiling on a grand scale, which ultimately harms the United States' global reputation, but NewStandard also argues that some legitimate concerns were not raised about the deal, and they should have been. NewStandard is an independent online newspaper that ceased publishing in 2007.

NewStandard Staff, "Dubai Ports Shake-up Exposes Racism, Cronyism," *The NewStandard*, http://newstandardnews.net, February 24, 2006. Reproduced by permission.

As you read, consider the following questions:

1. What reason did Senator Chuck Schumer give for objecting to Dubai Ports World assuming control of six major American seaports?

2. What two drawbacks to pulling out of the Dubai Ports World deal were cited by Arab-American Institute president James Zogby?

3. How much did the United Arab Emirates donate to relief efforts in the wake of Hurricane Katrina? What is the authors' implication?

News that an Arab-owned company would assume control of several US seaports prompted outcry from politicians in both major parties over national security concerns. In the background, additional fears emerged when administration critics learned of the less-than-transparent process by which the deal met with easy approval.

Foreign Control of U.S. Ports

Last week [February 2006], the United Arab Emirates-owned company Dubai Ports World (DPW), took over a British company that currently manages six US ports. When news of the $6.8 billion deal—which has DPW poised to begin operating US ports on March 2—broke in the US media, several lawmakers noted that terrorists, including Al-Qaeda operatives, have been connected to the UAE.

Democratic and Republican members of Congress alike used arguments exaggerating both the extent to which the UAE has been connected to terrorism and the role its company, DPW, would play in inspecting cargo at the ports under its control. Senator Chuck Schumer (D-NY), for instance, repeatedly claimed the UAE has had a "nexus of involvement with terrorism" and also insisted DPW would be responsible for inspecting shipments entering US ports.

But many other countries, including the United States and the United Kingdom, have had far more known connections to Islamic terrorists, such as the provision of residence and even citizenship, access to weaponry, issuance of legal identification and the use of banks.

Dubai Ports World, one of the largest port operators in existence, already manages terminals in eleven countries, including the UAE. There have been no reported incidents of the Emirates' monarchy or DPW itself supporting terrorism.

Other foreign operators handle terminals at all of the six US ports DPW is poised take control of. Furthermore, DPW, like the [British company P&O] it is poised to acquire and the many other foreign companies doing business at the nation's seaports and airports, would not be in charge of security. That remains the purview of US law and border enforcement agencies.

Racial Profiling at a Corporate Level

In official statements and comments to reporters, a number of Arab-American groups and public figures accused concerned lawmakers of xenophobia [fear of foreigners] and said the immediate criticism sparked by the deal wouldn't have come about had the company not been owned by an Arab nation.

"The anti-Arab impetus behind these protests is impossible to ignore, certainly doesn't make us safer, and trumps any positive message our public-diplomacy efforts seek to portray," Arab-American Institute President James Zogby said in a statement Wednesday. "The concern we have is that if an ally of the United States like the UAE can be smeared in this manner, simply because it's an Arab country, then our relations with the broader Arab world may be irreparably damaged."

Zogby's comments were echoed by others, including the American-Arab Anti-Discrimination Committee (ADC) and the Council on American-Islamic Affairs (CAIR).

CAIR spokesperson Ibrahim Hooper told the *Baltimore Sun* that US political leaders were "falling over one another trying to determine who's going to have the most anti-Arab, most anti-Muslim attitude."

In a statement released by the Institute for Public Accuracy, ADC spokesperson Laila Al-Qatami charged: "Those who purport that ports can be securely run by a British company, but not an Arab one, are engaging in racial profiling on the corporate level."

Anti-Arab Paranoia Distracts from Shady Dealings

Still, other questions about the deal remain over the manner in which the port contract was approved. [In January 2006], the White House nominated a former DPW executive, David Sanborn, to head the US Maritime Administration, where he will oversee the country's seaports. His role in the acquisition approval is unclear.

[In February 2006], the Associated Press [AP] reported it had received confirmation that the administration and DPW reached a somewhat routine arrangement regarding the company's cooperation in future US investigations prior to the P&O stockholder vote. Experts consulted by the AP said the arrangement lacked safeguards typical of such understandings, including any insistence that the company keep paperwork in the United States.

The discord over the deal did not surprise [corporate watchdog organization] Corpwatch director Pratap Chatterjee, who explained his view of the problem to the Institute for Public Accuracy: "On the one hand, it's protectionist and racist to prevent this because the company is based in an Arab country. But there clearly are factors of government secrecy and cronyism involved in this, as with so much of what the US government does."

The Dubai Ports World Hysteria

Like most Americans, President Bush knew nothing, if you believe his tubdrummers, about the infamous plan to cede control of six major American seaports to the United Arab Emirates. Technically, a company called Dubai Ports World (DPW) will run the ports, but given that DPW is state owned, it's a distinction without a difference. If the deal goes through, an Islamic regime will control shipping on the eastern seaboard of the United States.

Bush isn't the only one who pleaded ignorance of the deal. Michael Chertoff, the ballyhooed minister of Homeland Security, also claimed hirelings kept him in the dark. What the president knew and when he knew it will remain a mystery, but whatever he knew, he knows enough now to threaten vetoing a suggested congressional measure to investigate the deal. This veto threat comes from a supposed conservative who naively thinks "Islam is peace" and who has never uncapped the veto pen during his five years in office. Not once has Bush seen a spending bill cross his desk that could be cut by a mere penny. But suddenly he sees a bill that merits the veto.

The Bush administration would put a despotic Islamic regime, whose potentates and bankers boast significant ties to al-Qaeda terrorists, in charge of American shipping. If that seems impossible, clearly it isn't. The deal is yet another plot, approved in secret, which would undermine American national security and sovereignty for the benefit of the transnational political and commercial plutocrats who manage government and business across the globe.

R. Cort Kirkwood,
The New American, *March 20, 2006.*

The Bush family's business ties to the United Arab Emirates and the extensive use of UAE ports and airspace for US military operations have drawn suspicion to what appears to be a fast and smooth approval for such a deal. The secret cabinet-level committee tasked with investigating security concerns involving foreign investments opted to forgo the standard 45-day review mandated in such arrangements.

Nevertheless, skeptical observers suggest, such criticisms more readily highlight shortcomings of existing US policy and politics than they expose a particular threat posed by Dubai Ports World. *Washington Post* columnist E.J. Dionne Jr. point[ed] out [in February 2006] that, until the DPW deal came to light, "most Americans had no idea that our government's process of approving foreign takeovers of American [assets] through the Committee on Foreign Investments was entirely secret."

A Deal Delayed

According to the White House, the president had not been involved in reviewing the deal between P&O and Dubai Ports; he learned of it only after news of the story broke, despite the Committee on Foreign Investment's mandate to seek explicit presidential approval.

Just the same, less than a month before DPW first sought US approval of the ports deal, the UAE sent $100 million in relief funds for victims of Hurricane Katrina.

With congressional leaders threatening legislation to prevent DPW from assuming control of the domestic terminals, President Bush has vowed to veto any such measure. Were Bush to follow through on the veto, it would be the only one used since he assumed power in 2001.

However, White House Deputy Chief of Staff Karl Rove told Fox News yesterday [February 23, 2006] that the administration is open to a delay in the deal, and DPW has expressed willingness to delay the acquisition of US ports until Washington backs the deal with more confidence.

Also yesterday, the State of New Jersey filed a lawsuit in federal court seeking to stop the DPW deal. The Port Authority of New York and New Jersey also said it would file a lawsuit on Friday [February 24, 2006] seeking to terminate the lease for management of its busy shipping center.

> "A charge of racism against the police is all one needs to get the attention of the ACLU, the Justice Department, or the editors of major newspapers."

Accusations of Racial Profiling Alienate Law Enforcement

Michael Nevin Jr.

In the following viewpoint, Michael Nevin Jr. argues that the amount of attention devoted to racial profiling—a practice that he claims has not been demonstrated to be either systematic or widespread—alienates law enforcement. He argues that police, fearing bad press, hesitate to follow their instincts, and the result is plummeting arrest rates, climbing crime rates, and reduced public safety. Michael Nevin Jr. is a third-generation California police officer.

As you read, consider the following questions:

1. Why does Nevin call racial profiling "an enigma"?
2. How many fewer drug charges did the New Jersey State Troopers file in 2000 than in 1988?

Michael Nevin Jr., "The Battle Over Racial Profiling," *Men's News Daily*, http://mensnewsdaily.com, March 22, 2004. Reproduced by permission of the author.

3. Why does Sergeant Carl Fabbri frequently ask suspected drug dealers and gang members if they are armed, even though he knows that they will—armed or not—answer in the negative?

Police officers from New Jersey to California face an unrelenting assault from anti-police activists. The battle being waged against the police is a well organized strategy involving multiple fronts. But the strongest weapon in the anti-police arsenal, able to cause the most damage and drive a wedge in police-community relations, is the baseless charge of systematic racial profiling.

The "Racial Profiling" Bogeyman

Undoubtedly, America has had to come to terms with her own *mea culpa* ["my fault"] regarding inequality and racial bigotry. However, even decades after the civil rights movement, American police officers have been left holding the bag. The fact that police departments around the country have gone to great lengths to hire and promote based on diversity is of no consequence. A charge of racism against the police is all one needs to get the attention of the ACLU [American Civil Liberties Union], the Justice Department, or the editors of major newspapers.

A few years back, the term racial profiling was devised to describe the practice where race is used as the primary factor in targeting criminal behavior. Racial profiling became the watchword of the day and a national phenomenon. Conspiracy theorists could not have dreamed up a more widespread epidemic as police critics from coast to coast complained of this deplorable plot. The political implications were staggering, and very few leaders in the highest levels of government are willing to question it today. [Former president] Bill Clinton, [former attorney general] Janet Reno, [president] George W. Bush, and [former attorney general] John Ashcroft have at least one thing in common: all launched crusades against this enigma. It's an enigma because empirical research has yet to prove that racial profiling, to the extent that it has been reported, even exists.

Police officers have an indispensable ally in their effort to spread the truth and repudiate the myth of racial profiling: Heather Mac Donald of the Manhattan Institute. As the author of "Are Cops Racist? How the War Against the Police Harms Black Americans," she explains how the junk science—first used to declare New Jersey State Troopers guilty of racial profiling—has been debunked. The 1999 study that ignited the controversy had major flaws and failed to establish a violator benchmark; that is, the rate of lawbreaking among a particular group. A subsequent study exonerated the troopers when it found that black drivers were stopped less than their speeding behavior would predict.

Demoralized Police

However, the demoralizing effect on the troopers continued to linger. Mac Donald cites the following statistics: "At the height of the drug war in 1988, the [New Jersey] troopers filed 7,400 drug charges from the turnpike, most of those from consent searches; in 2000, they filed 370 drug charges. . . . Murder jumped 65 percent in Newark, a major destination of drug traffickers, between 2000 and 2001."

Facts can get in the way of a good news story. The firestorm, fueled by media hype and politics, has yet to be doused by the truth. The California Penal Code now defines racial profiling, and officers are required by state law to participate in expanded training. An officer without a racist bone in his body sits in a classroom feeling like a guy who never drank attending an AA [Alcoholics Anonymous] meeting. It may be the classic example of a solution looking for a problem. In my

The Racial Profiling Myth

Heather Mac Donald: The studies that purport to prove the existence of racial profiling are junk science that wouldn't earn their authors an F in a freshman statistics course. . . .

An example: In New York, blacks are 50% of all persons stopped and frisked by the police, but only 25% of the population. Police critics seize on this disparity between population percentages and enforcement activity to charge the police with racism. And such a disparity would indeed be cause for concern if crime rates were evenly distributed across the population. They are not, however—not in New York, not anywhere. In New York, in 1998, 62% of victims of violent assault identified their assailants as black, meaning that blacks were 13 times more likely to commit a violent assault as whites. Remember: these are victims identifying the criminal, not the allegedly "racist" police. It turns out that blacks in New York are actually being under stopped, compared to their rates of violent crime. . . .

If we want the police to be effective, they must direct their enforcement activity based on crime, not on skin color.

John Hawkins,
"10 Questions with Heather Mac Donald,"
Right Wing News. *www.rightwingnews.com*

opinion, based on actual experience, the overwhelming majority of men and women entering law enforcement intend to harass criminals, not minorities.

Sergeant Carl Fabbri has worked in many of San Francisco's toughest neighborhoods. Currently working in the Bayview District, Sgt. Fabbri knows the "players," and the "players" know him. I asked him to weigh in on the matter, and here's what he had to say: "Police officers have a unique instinct, sometimes called a 'sixth sense,' that alerts us to danger. We rely on it to keep us alive. This 'sixth sense' is developed from years of experience dealing with thieves, drug dealers, parolees, and gang members. We frequently ask questions like 'Do you have any weapons on you?' We know the answer will be 'no' almost every time but that's not why we ask. We ask because it gives us an opportunity to see how they react to the question . . . to see their body language . . . to study their eyes. More often than not, our instincts are right on."

Fear of Accusations Prevents Taking Action

"Our profession is under intense scrutiny from coast to coast. Some cops are ignoring the warning signs, the 'sixth sense,' because they fear citizen complaints and lawsuits. Worse yet, some cops have taken the 'do nothing/do nothing wrong' attitude. Given the political climate we're working in, can you blame them? Criminals terrorizing the neighborhoods love to see the 'do nothing wrong' cops patrolling the neighborhoods. It doesn't take a criminologist to realize how the extreme scrutiny we're currently experiencing will result in increased crime rates and put officer safety in jeopardy."

"Since we hold the power to use deadly force and deprive people of their freedom, the work of police officers has to be scrutinized. There is no valid argument against police accountability. Unfortunately, the pendulum continues to swing too far to the left, and there's no sign of it swinging back anytime soon. The solution is unclear at this point. Restoring the public's confidence in our profession is our best option. This will only be accomplished by educating the public, political leaders, and the media on what's really going on in the trenches of the war on crime."

The collateral damage associated with the anti-racial profiling campaigns can be found in communities that can least afford it. Inner city, law-abiding citizens suffer when false information and racially charged rhetoric become the order of the day. Conspiracy theorists who came up empty trying to prove the racial profiling hypothesis may want to turn their focus toward those who profit from "de-policing" in America. Police officers and honest citizens could use the reprieve.

| *"Critics fear that the DNA sketch concept opens the door to biased, unscientific racial profiling based on unproven gene markers for behavior, including criminal behavior."*

Concerns About Racial Profiling Stifle Innovation in Law Enforcement Technology

Jessica Snyder Sachs

In the following viewpoint, Jessica Snyder Sachs explores advances in DNA forensics, which she claims is moving beyond simply identifying "matches" to providing a "sketch" of a suspect's appearance based solely on genetic information. Sachs argues that DNA evidence is underutilized because of ongoing concerns about racial profiling and the possibility of "DNA profiling" of citizens based solely on "genetic predisposition." Jessica Snyder Sachs is a science writer and the author of Good Germs, Bad Germs: Health and Survival in a Bacterial World *and* Corpse: Nature, Forensics, and the Struggle to Pinpoint Time of Death.

Jessica Snyder Sachs, "DNA and a New Kind of Racial Profiling," *Popular Science,* vol. 263, no. 6, December 1, 2003, pp. 16f. Copyright © 2003 Time, Inc. Reproduced by permission.

As you read, consider the following questions:

1. According to the author, why are genes that denote ancestral geographic origins not included among the genes officially used for DNA evidence matching in criminal cases?

2. Does the author claim it will ever be possible to reconstruct a suspect's face using only DNA evidence? Why or why not?

3. Why does Tony Frudakis believe his company, DNAPrint Genomics, will succeed where others, such as the British Forensic Science Service's DNA photofit project, failed?

Nothing in American police work is more controversial than racial profiling. Minorities are targeted for small offenses in the hope of uncovering bigger crimes, and the practice has generated successful lawsuits by the ACLU [American Civil Liberties Union] and pledges from state governments and law enforcement agencies to clean up their discriminatory acts.

What DNA Reveals About Appearance

Add to this charged atmosphere the prospect of a DNA-race angle. By now most Americans know that when criminals leave traces of themselves—blood, semen, hair, a scrape of skin under a victim's fingernails—at crime scenes, they leave a unique genetic fingerprint that can establish their presence at the scene with great certainty. Less known but more controversial is that DNA traces also leave clues about ancestry and appearance, clues that, as genetic science matures, might be used to generate a sort of police sketch.

Racial differences constitute small notes within the great opus of the human genetic code, but the very fact that genetic markers linked to ethnic origin are, in a sense, cosmetic—that is, they affect outward appearance—makes them potentially useful in the hunt for criminals. Is a suspect of fair Celtic stock or of darker African origin? His or her DNA may tell. Such information could prove far more useful to street-pounding cops than notoriously unreliable eyewitness reports. But unless the science proves reliable, there is risk here: The use of DNA markers could confer authority on police searches—isn't genetic information more reliable than even fingerprints?—that, in the area of racial markers and appearance, it may not deserve.

Until recently, genetic markers have not been used in manhunts, but that changed earlier this year [2003] when a private gene lab concluded that an unknown serial killer was a medium-to-dark-skinned black, not the white man that police had been focused on. The lab, it turned out, was correct, and although its conclusion did not directly lead to the arrest of the suspect, it advanced the case for supporters of the DNA sketch idea.

Deliberately Avoiding Race

In 1997, when members of the national DNA Advisory Board officially selected the gene markers for DNA evidence matching, they could have included a few markers associated with ancestral geographic origins (European, East Asian, sub-Saharan African)—which are a good indication of race and ethnicity. "We deliberately chose not to do so," says Ranajit Chakraborty, director of the University of Cincinnati's Center for Genome Information. Chakraborty says the board skirted the racial-marker issue in part because of the political minefield it represented. Thus today's standard American DNA fingerprint, with its battery of 15 gene markers (two were recently added to the standard 13), is a sort of bar code identifier that is fine for matching two DNA samples but offers no hints about the human package from which a crime-scene DNA sample is derived.

Not that DNA hasn't already been quietly used for ethnic identification. Following the 9/11 terrorist attacks, Chakraborty acceded to the request of a family whose son had been a passenger on United Flight 93 (the thwarted terrorist mission brought down in Pennsylvania). "We had a specimen that consisted of at least two individuals' remains, one of which was their son's," he explains. "The family was reluctant to bury it with his other body parts if it contained any remains that might belong to a hijacker." Chakraborty determined, with 95 percent certainty, that the unidentified tissue did not belong to anyone of Middle Eastern ancestry.

"We may not be able to tell German from French," says Chakraborty, "but we can place individuals in major continental groups." In turn, within each of these groups, certain types of hair texture, eye and skin color, and other facial features predominate. Such information could prove useful in an investigation, admits Chakraborty. "But [it] should not be interpreted that you can say with 100 percent accuracy that a person will have, say, brown eyes."

Because geneticists have largely kept mum about ethnic markers, it proved something of a shock when [private company] DNAPrint Genomics concluded last March [2003] that a Louisiana serial killer's "biogeographical ancestry" was 85 percent sub-Saharan African and 15 percent Native American. At the time, the police were on an altogether different track: They had been seeking a white man who had been seen lurking in the neighborhood of one of the crime scenes.

"Basically, the phone line went silent," says Tony Frudakis, research director at DNAPrint, describing the conference call in which he revealed the lab's results to police investigators. They were dubious, Frudakis says, and asked to see DNAPrint's analyses of 20 other DNA samples of known individuals they'd sent along with the killer's sample to test the lab's reliability. "We got them all right," Frudakis says.

The investigators were convinced enough to expand their search to include African-Americans, then had a break in the case due to an unrelated incident. Derrick Todd Lee, called in

Refusing to Embrace the Technology

[Tony Frudakis of DNAPrint Genomics] has identified the gene sequences associated with height, and has compiled a database of 5000 digital photographs of people with almost every racial ancestry combination—which, one day, he says could allow him to construct a physical portrait of a DNA donor, including melanin content, skin color or eye color.

But even the people one might think should be his biggest allies aren't supporting that, including Tony Clayton, the special prosecutor who tried one of the Baton Rouge murder cases [against the African-American serial killer Derrick Todd Lee]. Clayton, who is black, admits that he initially dismissed Frudakis as some white guy trying to substantiate his racist views. He no longer believes that and says "had it not been for Frudakis, we would still be looking for the white guy in the white pick-up truck." But then he adds, "We've been taught that we're all the same, that we bleed the same blood. If you subscribe to the (Frudakis) theory, you're saying we are inherently unequal."

He continues: "If I could push a button and make this technology disappear, I would."

Melba Newsome,
"The Inconvenient Science of Racial DNA Profiling,"
Wired.com, *October 5, 2007. www.wired.com*

for questioning about two unrelated killings, voluntarily gave a DNA sample, which police say matched DNA from the serial murders. Arrested on May 27 and now awaiting trial, Lee is African-American. [Lee was convicted in 2004.]

A History of DNA Dead Ends

A basic ancestry profile may be just the beginning for the DNA-based police sketch, boosters say. "To be honest, most of us are mongrels," says Frudakis. "We reside somewhere along a continuum rather than as members of physically distinct groups." He says DNAPrint is developing genomic tests to detect more specific physical traits, and it hopes to have the first such test—Retinome, for eye color—ready for market by the end of 2003. "After that, give us another year for hair color," he says. The latter is a particularly bold boast, since not much is known about hair color markers beyond one associated with red hair.

DNAPrint is not the first to claim progress toward a gene-based police sketch. In the late 1990s, Britain's Forensic Science Service [a government owned company that provides forensic services to their police forces] trumpeted the development of something called a DNA photofit. Emboldened by the identification of the gene marker for the "Celtic look" (fair skin and red hair), it poured money into an ambitious project at University College London. Scientists scanned the faces of hundreds of volunteers in an attempt to correlate digitized facial geometry with genetic markers.

The approach made intuitive sense, and it would have closely paralleled the anthropometric tricks used by police sketch artists, who build their drawings around a witness's best recollections of certain landmark geometries, such as nose height and width, eye shape and the distance across the broadest part of the face.

The Forensic Science Service had faith that the University College team could deliver in a couple of years, says team member Alf Linney, a medical imaging expert at University College London. But the connection between genes and facial appearance proved too complex for the London scientists, and the project was suspended in 2000.

Promising Technology, Not Without Snags

"We may never be able to fully reconstruct a suspect's face from genes alone," says Mark Benecke, one of Germany's most respected forensic biologists. "Genes coordinate the whole thing, but events during development and illnesses or malnutrition during childhood greatly influence facial symmetry." As every high school biology student learns, genotype plus environment equals phenotype—the physical expression of our genes. All of which Frudakis concedes. Still, he argues that the sophistication of new "high-throughput" computer analysis of genetic information greatly expands the layers of genetic clues that can go into a DNA-based best guess about a person's physical appearance.

"We're using neural networks and sophisticated pattern detection methodology to systematically determine genetic sequences over the whole genome for thousands of people," Frudakis says. "So when we're searching for genes associated with hair color, in essence we're doing a grid search. It's a treasure hunt in which we systematically determine, OK, the treasure isn't here, let's search the next grid." This contrasts, he says, with gene searches of just a few years ago, which were much more hit-and-miss.

Critics fear that the DNA sketch concept opens the door to biased, unscientific racial profiling based on unproven gene markers for behavior, including criminal behavior. "The temptation will be to run DNA data through computers to conclude, for example, that you can identify markers for, say, sexual offenders," warns sociologist Troy Duster, author of *Backdoor to Eugenics* and a consultant to the National Human Genome Research Institute. Imagine such a data crunch based on the DNA of convicted criminals, given the preponderance of black and Hispanic men in American prisons. "It would be like going to the NFL and concluding that the DNA marker for sickle-cell anemia [associated with African ancestry] makes you a good football player."

Despite such objections, forensic biologists like Benecke predict that the accuracy of DNA-based descriptions will edge past that of eyewitness accounts within 15 years, barring legal roadblocks. Germany currently outlaws the disclosure of DNA-gleaned information, except in medical situations with a patient's consent. "Technically, we're not even supposed to notice if there's a Y [male] chromosome," says Benecke. "But how can it be an invasion of privacy if we're only looking at things that can be seen from the outside?"

Unencumbered by such privacy laws, U.S. forensic labs already have nearly everything they need to develop their own "genetic witnesses." Given the time and money, they will continue with the genomic sifting and sorting. Frudakis makes this bold prediction: "A few years from now, we're going to have figured out so many traits that a criminal might as well leave his driver's license at the scene of the crime."

"Public perception relating to the use of
force by law enforcement, particularly
toward minorities, does not mirror reality."

The Specter of Racial Profiling Obstructs Law Enforcement

Steve Holbert and Lisa Rose

*In the following viewpoint, Steve Holbert and Lisa Rose explore
the public perception of racial profiling. They argue that while
the public believes police regularly practice racial profiling and
treat minority suspects roughly, statistics do not support the public perception. According to the authors, police apply force in less
than 1 percent of their interactions with the public, and most often against white males, who also are more likely than minority
members to be injured during these incidents. Lisa Rose is an attorney who has extensively researched racial profiling. Steve Holbert is a 30-year police veteran and a California state-certified
racial profiling instructor.*

Steve Holbert and Lisa Rose, *The Color of Guilt & Innocence: Racial Profiling and Police
Practices in America*, San Ramon, California: Page Marque Press, 2008, pp. 103–107.

As you read, consider the following questions:

1. What portion of young black men aged eighteen to thirty-four believe they have been stopped by police because of their race?

2. What percentage of police officers believe that white suspects are treated better than minority suspects?

3. According to the authors, how often does police use of force result in an injury?

In December 1999, a Gallup Poll reported that most Americans, particularly young black men, view racial profiling as extensive. The race of those surveyed seemed to be a predominant factor in the study's results, with 77% of black respondents believing that racial profiling is widespread, compared with 56% of whites. Though racial profiling allegations tend to be more prevalent among those living in urban areas than those in suburban areas or rural America, the report reflects few regional differences in the *perception* of the incidences of racial profiling. Regardless of how closely these beliefs mirror reality, one cannot ignore the study's finding that an overwhelming 81% of Americans, both white and black, disapprove of the practice.

Self-Reports of Profiling Are Distressingly Common

To understand the source of this discontent better, Americans were asked whether they felt the police had ever stopped them just because of their race or ethnic background. More than four out of ten blacks responded "yes." Moreover, about six out of ten who reported being stopped because of their race said it had occurred three or more times, including 15% who said it had happened eleven or more times.

The study revealed that almost three-quarters of *young* black men aged 18–34 were the individuals most likely to report being stopped by police because of their race. Comparatively, only 40% of young black women perceived themselves to have been the victims of racial profiling. An even smaller percentage of both black men and women aged 50 and older reported being stopped because of their race, a fact that left many to surmise that age and gender play a significant role in this practice.

Similar patterns were apparent when black men and women were asked how local police, state police, and police in other states treated them. The largest sense of unfair treatment was among young black men, particularly with respect to treatment by local police. For example, 53% of black men between the ages of 18 and 34 reported unfair treatment by their local law enforcement. That number dropped significantly to 23% of black men between the ages of 35 and 49 who felt that they were not treated fairly and 22% for those over 50. Comparatively, among black women between the ages of 18 and 34, 26% felt that they were treated unfairly. This number dropped to 19% for those 35 to 49 and fell to 18% for those aged 50 and over. Perceptions of unfair treatment were less pronounced among these groups when asked how they felt about treatment by their state police.

Consistent with the suspicions of many minorities, the study suggests that education and income seem to be a negligible factor in this equation. Well-educated, higher-income blacks are as likely to report being pulled over as those with lower levels of education and income. Some theorize that factors of wealth or success may have a direct correlation to the lucrative nature of the drug trade, thus causing young men in high-profile cars to appear more suspicious to police. . . .

Officers Also Believe Profiling Is Common

We know what the public thinks, but what do line officers think about allegations of racism in their profession? One study included in a report by the Christopher Commission in Los Angeles [headed by attorney Warren Christopher in the

"You don't have to be racist to work here, but if you are I don't suppose anyone will notice," cartoon by Clive Goddard, www.CartoonStock.com.

wake of the 1991 beating of Rodney King] indicated that 25% of 650 officers responding agreed that "racial bias (prejudice) on the part of officers toward minority citizens currently exists and contributes to a negative interaction between police and the community ... [and more than 25% agreed that] an officer's prejudice toward the suspect's race may lead to the use of excessive force."

Both sides of the argument put a different spin on the statistics. The ACLU [American Civil Liberties Union] points to the numbers as a message to elected officials to "catch up with the voters and pass legislation to address this problem." Yet some in law enforcement point to these statistics as nothing more than evidence of an escalating crime problem in minority communities, with the disproportionate stops representing police efforts to combat the growing problem. These statistics become even more challenging to analyze given other variables, such as the vast shift in population many communities are experiencing.

In the state of California for example, data released by the U.S. Census Bureau report that non-Hispanic whites make up less than 50% of California's overall population. This population shift, attributed to the influx of immigrants from Asia, Mexico, the Middle East, and Central and South America in the past decade lead many to question whether the crime statistics reported are evidence of racial profiling or merely a reflection of a rapidly growing, diverse population.

When looking at the numbers for total arrests in diverse states such as California, law enforcement analysts point out that arrests for the race/ethnic groups of "White" and "Black" decreased while arrests for the race/ethnic groups of "Hispanic" and "Other" increased. Analysts defend these arrest statistics and note that the changes are consistent with the population growth among these race/ethnic groups.

Similar conclusions were reached by former San Francisco Police Department Chief Fred Lau in response to a study revealing that blacks and Latinos are more likely than whites to be searched when stopped in San Francisco. The study results, reported in May 2002, revealed that blacks were 3.5 times more likely than whites to be searched, with Latinos being searched at a rate almost three times that of whites. Although the study raised a red flag for many civil rights advocates, former Chief Lau insisted that the numbers were not the result of racial profiling but rather reflective of other "sociological factors."

Regardless of these strong opinions, experts in the field have yet to definitively determine how much of a factor race is in everyday policing. If the perceptions of police officers themselves are any indication, 17% of officers reported that they believed police treated whites better than blacks and other minorities. When black officers were asked the same question, however, 51% agreed that whites receive better treatment.

Police Use-of-Force Statistics Tell a Different Story

When the public thinks about police officers' use of force against citizens, most immediately recount videos of officers "caught in the act" by an unsuspecting passerby with a video camera. These amateur films that inundate the evening news would lead one to question how widespread the problem has become. The reality is that most Americans believe that the use of force by the police is a common practice. Most would be surprised to learn that this widely held belief is not supported by any statistics we could find on police use of force. In fact, contrary to media reports and public perception, police use force in slightly less than one percent of their encounters with the public. And, Department of Justice reports indicate that when the police do use force or the threat of force, it is more often directed against white males. In 1999 (the last year such statistics were available), a Department of Justice report revealed that law enforcement officers either used force or threatened to use force against about 422,000 citizens. Of this group, approximately 87% were males, and 13% were females. Contrary to widely held stereotypes, 59% of these citizens were white, and 23% were black. The report also indicated that the threat or use of force peaks at 37.5% among 20- to 29-year-olds and then declines steadily with increasing age. In summary, police officers refrained from using force or threats of force in 99.04% of all encounters with the public.

When force was used, about 40% of the cases resulted in injuries. More than half of those injuries were among whites. In use of force incidents by police, blacks reported injury in slightly more than 8% of the cases, compared with Hispanics who reported injury in 11% of the encounters and whites who reported injury in 20% of the incidents.

Consistent with these government statistics, one survey reflects that most police officers in the United States disapprove of the use of excessive force. In fact, only 4.1% of officers believed that police regularly used more force than necessary when arresting a suspect, with 97.1% reporting that instances similar to that occurring in the [1991] Rodney King [police beating] case in Los Angeles and the Abner Louima case [Louima was brutalized by New York City Police in 1997] in New York were "extremely rare" in their organizations.

Despite officers' disapproval of the use of force, more than 30% believed that they should be permitted to utilize more force than is currently permissible by law, with 25% agreeing that it may sometimes be necessary to use more force than legally allowable to control a person who is physically assaulting an officer. More than 40% of the officers polled agreed that following their agencies' rules in this regard might be incompatible with the goal of getting their job done.

The Public Believes Police Brutality Is a Problem

Regardless of these statistics, the trend in public opinion implies that Americans are becoming less tolerant of police using any degree of force, even in self-defense. In 1973, Americans were asked, "Are there any situations you can imagine in which you would approve of a policeman striking an adult male citizen?" Nationwide, 73% of Americans responded "yes." By 2000, the Department of Justice reported that the number of citizens answering this question in the affirmative dropped to 64%. In 1973, Americans were asked, "Would you approve of a police officer striking a citizen who was attacking the officer with his fists?" Ninety-seven percent of those responding answered "yes" in 1973 compared with 90% who answered in the affirmative in 2000.

Although this study was not specifically designed to answer questions relating to the occurrence of racial profiling and violence against minorities by the police, one can infer that public perception relating to the use of force by law enforcement, particularly toward minorities, does not mirror reality. These flawed perceptions may be due, in part, to media reports sensationalizing accounts of white cops beating up black suspects without any apparent provocation. Perhaps these stories are deemed more newsworthy than the victimization of a white suspect by the police or, even rarer, a case in which a minority officer inflicted the harm. When armed with these images, any attempt by law enforcement to make even legitimate stops against minorities may be thwarted from the outset because of the underlying bias and animosity that inevitably taint the interactions between law enforcement and the community. Moreover, when an officer observes a person's anxiety and hesitation during a citizen encounter, it may be misconstrued as guilt and may set in motion a process that will reinforce the negative biases each side possesses about the other.

> *"The [Bush] administration's post-9/11 campaign of ethnic and religious profiling sparked widespread resentment, especially in the countries whose nationals were targeted by the program— the very countries we need to work most closely with."*

Racial Profiling Has Needlessly Complicated the War on Terror

David Cole and Jules Lobel

In the following viewpoint, David Cole and Jules Lobel claim that current U.S. tactics in fighting terrorism—including the use of racial profiling—are actually crippling those efforts and fueling terrorist propaganda. Cole and Lobel argue that racial profiling erodes trust and generates resentments that undercut cooperation, both in local law enforcement and international relations. David Cole and Jules Lobel are law professors and the authors of Less Safe, Less Free: Why America Is Losing the War on Terror.

David Cole and Jules Lobel, *Less Safe, Less Free: Why America Is Losing the War on Terror*, New York City: The New Press, 2007, pp. 139–144. Copyright © 2007 by David Cole and Jules Lobel. All rights reserved. Reproduced by permission of The New Press, www.thenewpress.com. (800) 233-4830.

As you read, consider the following questions:

1. What do the authors say is the primary difference between Muslim populations in Great Britain and the United States?

2. According to the authors, what do former Central Intelligence Agency (CIA) director Stansfield Turner and former CIA Counterterrorism Center deputy chief Paul Pillar agree is essential to winning the war on terror?

3. According to the authors, what is the significance of a rural Saudi boy having pictures on his cell phone of the abuses committed by U.S. soldiers staffing the Abu Ghraib prison?

The deepest and most long-lasting consequence of the sacrifices we have made in the name of the preventive paradigm [strategy for fighting terrorism] is to the legitimacy of the struggle against terrorism itself. Once a leading exponent of the rule of law, the United States is now widely viewed as a systematic and arrogant violator of the most basic norms of human rights law—including the prohibitions against torture, disappearances, and arbitrary detention. That loss of legitimacy in turn makes us more vulnerable to terrorist attacks, as it makes cooperation with others in our defense more difficult and fuels the animus [hate] and resentment that inspire the attacks against us in the first place. As the bipartisan 9/11 Commission [created by Congress to investigate the causes of the terrorist attacks] recognized, the fight against terrorism is fundamentally a struggle for hearts and minds. There is no alternative, because there is no way to build a fortress that will repel all terrorist attacks. By throwing aside fundamental precepts of the rule of law the preventive paradigm [strategy] makes it that much more difficult for the United States to appeal to the hearts and minds of those who might turn against us. . . .

Fostering Trust in Arab and Muslim Communities

Because it so radically challenges basic commitments to the rule of law, the preventive paradigm is likely to erode trust in government at the very moment when trust is most needed. Trust is particularly essential during a military conflict or other national security crisis. In such periods, the government by necessity cannot share all the information it has about the threat that it faces, but at the same time needs the support of the population in mobilizing an effective response. The only way to obtain that support without being able to show in detail the nature of the threat is by building trust. But when the [Bush] administration is shown time and time again to have pursued initiatives of questionable legitimacy, and to have broadly invoked secrecy to evade accountability, trust will inevitably erode.

Nowhere is the maintenance of trust more important than in Arab and Muslim communities within the United States. Given al-Qaeda's ideological commitments and ethnic makeup, al-Qaeda operatives are likely to seek support from these communities, as did the al-Qaeda leader who convinced the young men from Lackawanna, New York, to attend an al-Qaeda training camp. Our law enforcement agents need to work closely with Arab and Muslim communities if they are to develop the intelligence necessary to identify, monitor, and counteract potential threats therein. But if members of these communities feel that they have been unfairly targeted in a broad-brush way for little more than their ethnic and religious identities, cooperation will be difficult. As Sadullah Khan, director of the Islamic Center of Irvine, California, told the *Washington Post* in 2007, "How much cooperation can we give . . . at the same time we ourselves are part of the problem in [their] eyes?"

The sweeping roundups and widespread profiling conducted in the first two years after 9/11, coupled with the continuing perception that authorities have selectively directed a

What are America's Motives in the War on Terror?

About half of respondents in the four Muslim countries surveyed—and roughly four-in-ten in France and Germany—say the U.S. is conducting the war on terrorism to target unfriendly Muslim governments and groups.

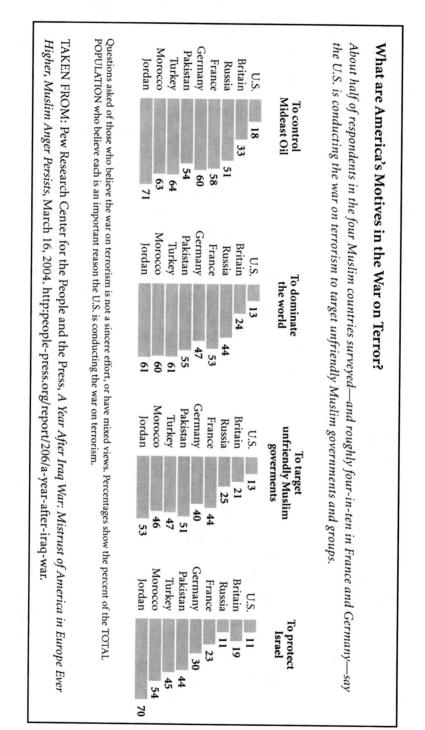

To control Mideast Oil

U.S.	18
Britain	33
Russia	51
France	58
Germany	60
Pakistan	54
Turkey	64
Morocco	63
Jordan	71

To dominate the world

U.S.	13
Britain	24
Russia	44
France	53
Germany	47
Pakistan	55
Turkey	61
Morocco	60
Jordan	61

To target unfriendly Muslim governments

U.S.	13
Britain	21
Russia	25
France	44
Germany	40
Pakistan	51
Turkey	47
Morocco	46
Jordan	53

To protect Israel

U.S.	11
Britain	19
Russia	11
France	23
Germany	30
Pakistan	44
Turkey	45
Morocco	54
Jordan	70

Questions asked of those who believe the war on terrorism is not a sincere effort, or have mixed views. Percentages show the percent of the TOTAL POPULATION who believe each is an important reason the U.S. is conducting the war on terrorism.

TAKEN FROM: Pew Research Center for the People and the Press, *A Year After Iraq War: Mistrust of America in Europe Ever Higher, Muslim Anger Persists,* March 16, 2004. http:people-press.org/report/206/a-year-after-iraq-war.

zero-tolerance policy at their communities ever since, have made Arabs and Muslims understandably nervous about coming forward. As Britain has learned, the cost of distrust is not merely in foregone intelligence; the British were shocked to learn that the July 7, 2005 [London subway] suicide bombers were young men born and raised in Great Britain itself. The Arab and Muslim population in the United States is as a general matter more integrated and less alienated than their counterparts in Europe, but that fact only underscores the opportunities federal officials have squandered by treating these communities as suspect.

Profiling Spoils International Cooperation

The negative consequences of illegitimate initiatives are not limited to a divided domestic polity [population]. There can be little doubt that the administration's "war on terror" has radically undermined the United States' standing throughout the world. Even before the administration launched its preventive war against Iraq, much of the world had come to view the United States' actions in the war on terror with deep skepticism and antagonism. A Pew Research poll conducted in 2002 found that 80 percent of French citizens, 85 percent of Germans, 68 percent of Italians, and 73 percent of the British felt that the United States was acting mainly in its own interest in the war on terror, while only small minorities thought the United States was taking into account the views of its allies. Another 2002 study found that favorable attitudes toward the United States had fallen in nineteen of twenty-seven countries polled. More than half of the people in all of the following countries felt that U.S. foreign policy did not consider the interests of others: Canada, Great Britain, Italy, France, Poland, Ukraine, Czech Republic, Slovak Republic, Russia, Bulgaria, Jordan, Lebanon, Egypt, Turkey, Mexico, Brazil, Argentina, Japan, South Korea, and Senegal. Majorities in Jordan, Lebanon, Egypt, Turkey, Indonesia, South Korea, and Senegal opposed the U.S.-led war on terror.

The cause of these reactions—even before the Iraq War—is no mystery. Foreign press and foreign governments alike have been highly critical of many of the administration's coercive preventive measures, most of which have, after all, been selectively targeted at foreign nationals and expressly defended on that ground. It would be difficult to name a single country, friend or foe, that has *not* criticized the mistreatment of detainees at Guantánamo [U.S. detention camp in Cuba] and in Iraq. Similarly, the [Bush] administration's post-9/11 campaign of ethnic and religious profiling sparked widespread resentment, especially in the countries whose nationals were targeted by the program—the very countries we need to work most closely with.

To fight an international foe like al-Qaeda, we need international cooperation. We do not have the resources, contacts, or cultural expertise to identify and assess risks that might arise in any of literally dozens of nations around the world. Yet because an attack could be planned and launched from almost anywhere, we need to develop wide-ranging intelligence. The only way to do that is to work with the citizenry and intelligence agencies of other nations. For this reason, both Stansfield Turner, former director of Central Intelligence, and Paul Pillar, former deputy chief of the CIA's Counterterrorism Center, have argued that success in countering terrorism critically depends on fostering strong relationships with foreign governments and intelligence agencies. Strong relationships—with governments, their intelligence agents, or ordinary citizens—depend on trust. And trust is precisely what is lost when the United States is viewed as acting illegitimately, in particular toward Arabs and Muslims.

U.S. Actions Set the Tone Around the World

Disregarding basic principles of the rule of law also provides cover for other nations that may be only too happy to follow suit, and that in turn can raise security costs for the United States. As Human Rights Watch has reported in its annual World Reports, since 9/11 many repressive regimes around the world have used the United States' shortcuts in the war on terror as license to adopt their own harshly coercive measures, often directed not at terrorists but at dissidents or opposition parties. Such repression invariably breeds resentment among those targeted or those associated with the targeted groups, and increases the likelihood that the opposition will turn to violent means. Moreover, to the extent that a nation's repressive measures are seen as linked to the United States, it plays into the hands of the propaganda of al-Qaeda and other violent extremists who seek to portray the United States as responsible for repression far beyond its borders.

Perhaps most fundamentally, when we sacrifice legitimacy, we drive bystanders into the terrorists' camp. Terrorists cannot hope to win a straight-out military struggle, so they instead fight an ideological battle. Their attacks are designed to trigger overreaction from the nation under attack, and they then use that overreaction to garner support for their cause. . . . That young [rural Saudi Arabian] children are now carrying images of [prisoner torture from U.S.-run] Abu Ghraib around on their cell phones points to the fallacy of the preventive paradigm; when we sweep away the rules in the name of preventing the next attack, we foster the conditions that make the next attack that much more likely.

Periodical Bibliography

The following articles have been selected to supplement the diverse views presented in this chapter.

Adrian Castañeda — "When Americans Get Deported Illegally," *Santa Barbara Independent*, July 23, 2008.

CBCNews — "U.S. Legislators Apologize to Maher Arar," October 19, 2007. http://www.cbc.ca/world/story/2007/10/18/arar.html.

David Cole — "How Not to Fight Terrorism," *Washington Post*, May 5, 2006.

Richard L. Davis — "The Causes and Consequences Of Racial Profiling," *Men's News Daily*, August 10, 2004.

Bill Dedman and Francie Latour — "Race, Sex, and Age Drive Ticketing," *Boston Globe*, July 20, 2003.

Jack McDevitt and Lisa Bailey — "Looking Deeper at Racial Profiling," *Boston Globe*, August 2, 2003.

Ontario Human Rights Commission — "Paying the Price: The Human Cost of Racial Profiling," October 21, 2003. http://www.ohrc.on.ca/en/resources/discussion_consultation/RacialProfileReportEN/view.

Pew Research Center for the People and the Press — "A Year After Iraq War: Mistrust of America in Europe Ever Higher, Muslim Anger Persists," March 16, 2004. http://people-press.org/report/206/a-year-after-iraq-war.

Leah Lakshmi Piepzna-Samarasinha — "Even in Canada: A High-Profile Government Sting That Targeted 24 South Asian Men Has Set Off National Controversy and a Vibrant, Immigrant-Led Defense," *Colorlines Magazine*, Fall 2004.

Matt Sanctis — "Police, Sheriff Discuss Racial Profiling Practices," *Springfield News-Sun*, May 9, 2008.

Jacqueline Stevens — "Thin ICE," *The Nation*, June 5, 2008.

For Further Discussion

Chapter 1

1. The American Civil Liberties Union (ACLU) and Heather Mac Donald make opposite claims about the existence of racial profiling. The ACLU's argument relies on a large number of anecdotes, while Mac Donald's is based on traffic-stop and arrest statistics. Which argument do you find more persuasive? Why?

2. Ilya Somin argues that racial profiling and affirmative action are essentially the same, because they both make judgments based on apparent race. Austin Cline does not question this assertion but rather argues that, because racial discrimination is generally founded in hate and affirmative action is founded in an attempt to help, the two are fundamentally different. Do the good intentions inherent in affirmative action negate the seeming wrong of using race to judge someone? Why or why not?

3. Both Jonathan V. Last and Eric Lipton quote Israeli security expert Rafi Ron. Based on these quotes, do you believe Rafi Ron would approve of behavioral profiling as it is implemented in U.S. airports? Explain.

Chapter 2

1. Daniel Pipes argues that it is vital to profile Muslims in fighting the war on terror, because contemporary terrorism is part of a holy war declared by radical, extremist Muslims. Richard Miniter, Mark Engler, and Saurav Sarkar argue that such profiling violates the law, is unethical, and is a waste of resources. If Muslims could be profiled efficiently, would it be acceptable to ignore the legal and ethical concerns? Why or why not?

2. Which do you think is a greater cause for concern: the Immigration and Naturalization Service registering Arab Muslim men (as described by Engler and Sarkar) or the day-to-day suspicion businesses show toward Muslims (as described by Michael Scherer)?

Chapter 3

1. Based on the viewpoints and inserts presented in this chapter, do you believe that it was necessary for the United States to imprison Japanese Americans during World War II? If you believe that imprisonment was going too far, would it have made sense to subject Japanese Americans to heightened scrutiny, based on the information available at the time? If so, how much extra scrutiny would have been appropriate?

2. Based on the viewpoints written by Sally Satel and Robert Lee Hotz, do you believe that doctors should take race into account when making a diagnosis? Why or why not?

Chapter 4

1. Do you believe that concerns about American shipping ports being operated by Dubai Ports World (and thus the government of the United Arab Emirates) were exaggerated? Why or why not?

2. Both Michael Nevin Jr. and Heather Mac Donald, whom he quotes, claim that police are actually fighting crime less aggressively in black communities because of fears they will be accused of racial profiling. Which do you believe would be more detrimental to a minority community: the perception that police single them out, or the perception that laws can be broken with no repercussions?

Organizations to Contact

The editors have compiled the following list of organizations concerned with the issues debated in this book. The descriptions are derived from materials provided by the organizations. All have publications or information available for interested readers. The list was compiled on the date of publication of the present volume; the information here may change. Be aware that many organizations take several weeks or longer to respond to inquiries, so allow as much time as possible.

American Civil Liberties Union (ACLU)
125 Broad St., 18th Floor, New York, NY   10004
(212) 549-2500
e-mail: aclu@aclu.org
Web site: www.aclu.org

The American Civil Liberties Union works to preserve freedoms of expression and religious practice, and rights to privacy, due process, and equal protection under the law. It provides free legal services to those whose rights have been violated. The ACLU Web site offers an array of policy statements, pamphlets, and fact sheets on civil rights issues.

Amnesty International USA
5 Penn Plaza, New York, NY   10001
(212) 807-8400 • fax: (212) 627-1451
e-mail: aimember@aiusa.org
Web site: www.amnestyusa.org

Founded in 1961, Amnesty International is a grassroots activist organization that aims to free all nonviolent people who have been imprisoned because of their beliefs, ethnic origin, race, or gender. Amnesty International USA makes its reports, press releases, and fact sheets available through its Web site, including the report *Threat and Humiliation: Racial Profiling, National Security, and Human Rights in the United States.*

Cato Institute

1000 Massachusetts Ave. NW, Washington, DC   20001-5403
(202) 842-0200 • fax: (202) 842-3490
e-mail: cato@cato.org
Web site: www.cato.org

The Cato Institute is a libertarian public policy research foundation dedicated to limiting the role of government and protecting individual liberties. It publishes the quarterly magazine *Regulation*, the bimonthly *Cato Policy Report*, and numerous policy papers and articles.

Center for Immigration Studies

1522 K St. NW, Suite 820, Washington, DC   20005-1202
(202) 466-8185 • fax: (202) 466-8076
e-mail: center@cis.org
Web site: www.cis.org

The Center for Immigration Studies is a nonprofit institute dedicated to research and analysis of the economic, social, and demographic impacts of immigration on the United States. Founded in 1985, the center aims to expand public support for immigration policy that is both pro-immigrant and low-immigration. The center's research and reports are available on its Web site.

Citizens' Commission on Civil Rights (CCCR)

2000 M St. NW, Suite 400, Washington, DC   20036
(202) 659-5565 • fax: (202) 223-5302
e-mail: citizen@cccr.org
Web site: www.cccr.org

CCCR is a bipartisan organization that monitors the federal government's enforcement of anti-discrimination laws and works to accelerate progress in the area of race relations and on other civil rights issues. It publishes books, and posts several annual reports online.

Council on American-Islamic Relations (CAIR)
453 New Jersey Ave. SE, Washington, DC 20003
(202) 488-8787 • fax: (202) 488-0833
e-mail: info@cair.com
Web site: www.cair.com

The Council on American-Islamic Relations is a Muslim civil liberties and advocacy group focused on both bridging the gap between Muslim and non-Muslim Americans, and protecting the rights of Muslims in the United States. CAIR regularly meets and works with law enforcement, and members of the federal, state, and local governments in order to facilitate communication with U.S. Muslim communities and raise awareness of issues affecting Muslims. The CAIR Web site includes reports, surveys, public service announcements, and press releases on both issues of specific concern to American Muslims, and on Islam-related topics of general interest.

Federal Bureau of Investigation (FBI)
935 Pennsylvania Ave. NW, Washington, DC 20535-0001
(202) 324-3000
Web site: www.fbi.gov

The FBI is the principal investigative arm of the U.S. Department of Justice. It investigates violations of federal criminal law, protects the United States from foreign intelligence and terrorist activities, and provides leadership and law enforcement assistance to federal, state, local, and international agencies. Press releases, congressional statements, major speeches on issues concerning the FBI, and crime statistics are available on the agency's Web site.

Manhattan Institute for Policy Research
52 Vanderbilt Ave., New York, NY 10017
(212) 599-7000 • fax: (212) 599-3494
e-mail: mi@manhattan-institute.org
Web site: www.manhattan-institute.org

The Manhattan Institute for Policy Research is a conservative think tank that supports economic choice and individual responsibility. The institute publishes a quarterly magazine, *City*

Journal, that advocates conservative, free-market urban policy. Many articles, interviews, policy papers, and reports written by the institute's fellows are available on its Web site.

National Association for the Advancement of Colored People (NAACP)
4805 Mt. Hope Dr., Baltimore, MD   21215
(877) 622-2798
Web site: www.naacp.org

Founded one hundred years ago, the NAACP is the oldest civil rights organization in the United States. Its primary focus is the protection and enhancement of the civil rights of African Americans and other minorities. Working at the national, regional, and local level, the organization educates the public on the adverse effects of discrimination; advocates legislation; and monitors enforcement of existing civil rights laws. The organization publishes *Crisis,* a bimonthly magazine, and provides press releases on its Web site.

National Urban League
120 Wall St., New York, NY   10005
(212) 558-5300 • fax: (212) 344-5332
e-mail: info@nul.org
Web site: www.nul.org

A community service agency, the National Urban League's mission is to eliminate institutional racism in the United States. It also provides services for minorities who experience discrimination in employment, housing, welfare, and other areas. The National Urban League publishes the report *The Price: A Study of the Costs of Racism in America,* the annual *State of Black America,* and other reports.

U.S. Department of Homeland Security (DHS)
Washington, DC   20528
(202) 282-8000
Web site: www.dhs.gov

Created in 2002 following the September 11, 2001, terrorist attacks, the DHS serves as a coordinating agency providing information about potential threats to the United States and its citizens, as well as offering tactical options to take action and prevent further harmful actions. Publications such as "Commitment to Race Neutrality in Law Enforcement Activities" are available on the Web site.

U.S. Department of Justice (DOJ)
950 Pennsylvania Ave. NW, Washington, DC   20530-0001
(202) 514-2000
e-mail: AskDOJ@usdoj.gov
Web site: www.usdoj.gov/

The mission of the DOJ is to enforce the law and defend the interests of the United States according to the law; to ensure public safety against threats foreign and domestic; to provide federal leadership in preventing and controlling crime; to seek just punishment for those guilty of unlawful behavior; and to ensure fair and impartial administration of justice for all Americans. Reports available on its Web site include "Guidance Regarding the Use of Race by Federal Law Enforcement Agencies," as well as articles about current DOJ activities and links to DOJ agencies such as the Civil Rights Division.

Bibliography of Books

Rebecca M. Blank, Marilyn Dabady, and Constance Forbes Citro
Measuring Racial Discrimination. Washington, DC: National Academies Press, 2004.

Charles L. Briggs
Stories in the Time of Cholera: Racial Profiling During a Medical Nightmare. Berkeley: University of California Press, 2004.

Michael K. Brown et al.
Whitewashing Race: The Myth of a Color-Blind Society. Berkeley: University of California Press, 2005.

John L. Burris and Catherine Whitney
Blue vs. Black: Let's End the Conflict Between Cops and Minorities. New York: St. Martin's Press, 2000.

Carl Cohen and James P. Sterba
Affirmative Action and Racial Preference: A Debate (Point/Counterpoint Series). New York: Oxford University Press, 2003.

Theodore Dalrymple
In Praise of Prejudice: The Necessity of Preconceived Ideas. New York: Encounter Books, 2007.

Alejandro Del Carmen
Racial Profiling in America. Upper Saddle River, NJ: Prentice Hall, 2007.

Darin D.   *Racial Profiling: Eliminating the Con-*
Fredrickson and   *fusion Between Racial and Criminal*
Raymond P.   *Profiling and Clarifying What Consti-*
Siljander   *tutes Unfair Discrimination and Perse-*
                          cution. Springfield, IL: Charles C.
                          Thomas, 2002.

Mary Matsuda   *Looking Like the Enemy: My Story of*
Gruenewald   *Imprisonment in Japanese American*
                          Internment Camps. Troutdale, OR:
                          NewSage Press, 2005.

Vikas K. Gumbhir   *But Is It Racial Profiling?: Policing,*
                          Pretext Stops, and the Color of Suspi-
                          cion. New York: LFB Scholarly Publi-
                          cations, 2007.

David A. Harris   *Profiles in Injustice: Why Racial Profil-*
                          ing Cannot Work. New York: W.W.
                          Norton, 2003.

Milton Heumann   *Good Cop, Bad Cop: Racial Profiling*
and Lance Cassak   *and Competing Views of Justice in*
                          America. New York: Peter Lang Pub-
                          lishing, 2003.

John I. Hogan   *Turnpike Trooper: Racial Profiling &*
                          the New Jersey State Police. Philadel-
                          phia: Xlibris, 2005.

Peter Irons   *Justice at War: The Story of the*
                          Japanese-American Internment Cases.
                          Berkeley: University of California
                          Press, 1993.

Annie Jacobsen   *Terror in the Skies: Why 9/11 Could*
                          Happen Again. Dallas, TX: Spence
                          Publishing Company, 2005.

Juan Antonio Juarez   *Brotherhood of Corruption: A Cop Breaks the Silence on Police Abuse, Brutality, and Racial Profiling.* Chicago: Chicago Review Press, 2004.

Randall Kennedy   *Race, Crime, and the Law.* New York: Vintage Books, 1998.

Alan B. Krueger   *What Makes a Terrorist: Economics and the Roots of Terrorism.* Princeton, NJ: Princeton University Press, 2007.

David D. Lowman   *MAGIC: The Untold Story of U.S. Intelligence and the Evacuation of Japanese Residents from the West Coast during WW II.* Twickenham, UK: Athena Press, 2000.

Heather Mac Donald   *Are Cops Racist?* Chicago: Ivan R. Dee Publisher, 2003.

Michelle Malkin   *In Defense of Internment: The World War II Round-Up and What It Means for America's War on Terror.* Washington, DC: Regnery Publishing, 2004.

Michelle Malkin   *Invasion: How America Still Welcomes Terrorists, Criminals, and Other Foreign Menaces to Our Shores.* Washington, DC: Regnery Publishing, 2004.

William McGowan   *Coloring the News: How Political Correctness Has Corrupted American Journalism.* New York: Encounter Books, 2003.

Kenneth Meeks   *Driving While Black: What to Do If You Are a Victim of Racial Profiling.* Louisville, KY: Broadway, 2000.

Mia Moody

Black and Mainstream Press' Framing of Racial Profiling: A Historical Perspective. Lanham, MD: University Press of America, 2008.

Sally Satel

PC, M.D.: How Political Correctness Is Corrupting Medicine. Jackson, TN: Basic Books, 2001.

Frederick Schauer

Profiles, Probabilities, and Stereotypes. Cambridge, MA: Belknap Press, 2006.

Michael A. Smerconish

Flying Blind. Philadelphia: Running Press, 2004.

Carol Tator and Frances Henry

Racial Profiling in Canada. Toronto: University of Toronto Press, 2006.

Brian L. Withrow

Racial Profiling: From Rhetoric to Reason. Upper Saddle River, NJ: Prentice Hall, 2005.

Index